CYBERSECURITY UNLOCKED!

Strategies To Outsmart Hackers, and Online Criminals

MILES LOCKHART

Contents

Part II
Defense Across All Dimensions Of Your Digital Life

Introduction

Food, shelter, and clothing.

We've long been taught that these three are the basic human needs. Certainly, it's hard to imagine life without these three.

Looking at the dynamics of the modern world, it's fair to say that the internet is a basic human need. Think about it for a moment, and let it sink in.

Imagine waking up one day, cut off from the internet. This might sound like a script from one of the post-apocalyptic movies, but mull over it a bit. This is not a periodic network outage, but there's no internet all over the world.

For most people, that's probably the end of the world. Imagine the magnitude of disruption that would befall our lives if this happened. Anyone who works online would effectively be jobless. You won't be able to access your bank account online. If you have money on platforms like PayPal, forget about ever getting it back. Communication networks would be disrupted. Social media would disappear. Transport networks would be massively affected, and so would access to crucial infrastructure.

Well, look at that. Our modern lives are hinged on the internet, so much so that not even a Spielberg movie could aptly capture the magnitude of what it means to live in a world without the internet. Thus, I'd stick my neck out and say the internet is a basic need, high up there with food, shelter, and clothing.

I would know, because I've spent more than 25 years working and interacting with people in the cybersecurity industry, with experience in crucial sectors of our economy. The mere thought of waking up to a world without the internet is perhaps as big a security threat as we'd ever imagine, but that can be addressed as a national security threat.

The interesting thing about cybersecurity that most people never realize is that it's usually the simple things we do that make a big difference. This is also true about life. How do you use your phone, your laptop, your TV, PlayStation, and so on? Most households today have at least one or more of these gadgets. Your use patterns and behavior will easily determine whether you become an easy target for cybercriminals or not.

I'll give you an interesting statistic—did you know that we experience thousands of new cybersecurity threats every day? To be precise, more than 4,000 new threats. This isn't meant to scare you, but it's the reality of the world we're living in.

Another reality is that there are cyber threats all around you each time you connect to the internet. So, the question you should be asking yourself is, how do you outsmart these threats? What can you do to stay safe online? Remember that cybercriminals are smart, and most of them have quite impressive tech setups capable of crippling national economies, so hacking into your laptop or your phone would be a walk in the park, right?

Security is a personal initiative. To be safe online, you must be intentional about it. You must take conscious steps to protect your online presence. I'm talking about your online banking accounts, social media, internet history, and so on. You must also protect your loved ones, who might be oblivious to the cyber threats around them, for example, kids, or your parents.

The good news is that you can do all that without necessarily enrolling in a cybersecurity course. Well, if you can, I'd encourage you to do so, as there's so much to learn about the cybersecurity infrastructure and the future of computing and integration in our lives.

That said, I'll draw your attention to simple, everyday things you can do to stay safe online. You'd be surprised, but you have available to you almost all the tools you need to protect yourself. You have random token generators like Google Authenticator, password managers, and password generators so you can stop using admin12345 as your network password, and so on.

Cyber threats are real, and people get hacked every day. While most people think of cyberattacks as an abrupt breach that causes chaos, this isn't always the case. If anything, most cyber-criminals quietly infiltrate your systems and build an entire ecosystem within yours, for their own nefarious reasons. They could install malware, hold your digital assets for ransom, execute the famous distributed denial of service (DDoS) attacks, and so on.

Cybercriminals could use you as their way into an organization they'd wish to hack. For example, if someone wanted to hack your employer, all they'd have to do is exploit security weaknesses in your phone or laptop, then sit and wait patiently for you to carry these devices to work, and just like that, your employer would be compromised. The problem here is that a security audit would trace the breach to you, which means there's a good chance you could lose your job for something you know nothing about. This isn't just an illustration, but it's an unfortunate reality that has destroyed the lives and livelihoods of lots of people all over the world.

The fact that there are threats all around us doesn't mean you should be afraid to come online and live a normal life. Data is the new gold, so it's equally important that you know how your data is being handled. Security online is as important as the measures you take to protect your household from intruders.

I believe that we'll have lots of engaging discussions in this book about online security, conversations that will help you protect all facets of your digital life. I'm talking about every-thing from digital finances, privacy, identity, communication, online work, your commute, or even private connections.

Your life is online, so you must do everything you can to protect it. I'm not creating an instruction manual, but instead, an easy conversation about a safe digital ecosystem, conversations that you can similarly have with your loved ones and not only awaken them to the dangers that lurk around them online but also share with them the tools they need to stay safe.

PART I

Unmasking The Digital Threatscape

"If you know the enemy and know yourself, you need not fear the result of a hundred battles."

Sun Tzu

First Things First - The Internet

What doesn't kill you makes you stronger…Kelly Clarkson once famously sang. The famous lyrics inspire hope and can help you build resilience against any adversities you're facing in life. Well, in the world of tech, none of that applies.

Even though tech threats might not kill you, the impact they'll have on your life is often so profound, that from a tech expert's perspective, I'd say tech threats essentially kill your identity online. Not to paint a grim picture or to scare you, but to be honest, cyber threats are just as dangerous as running into the neighborhood bully or a dreaded gang.

One of the biggest risks with cyber threats is that you never really know what the criminals are after, or their intentions. As we outlined in the Introduction, some cyber criminals aren't necessarily after you but could use you as a proxy to access their intended target.

But, where did this all start? Are humans always that bad?

Well, there are good and bad people online. That's just how life works. Bad people will exploit you, and they won't feel a thing. They'll just move on to the next target and hurt them as long as they can, and the cycle continues.

Trust, but verify. This is something I like to tell anyone who asks me about security online. If your instincts are jittery about something online, trust that feeling. Next, make a point to verify the information you come across online. Never take anything at face value.

Remember that time when you were writing your college term paper? There's a reason why your professors insist that you present an elaborate list of references, even though you did all the research on your own. For every factual statement you make, you must provide tangible evidence to back it up. That's what made your term paper authentic.

The same concept applies online. Even though no one is going to ask you for references, it's always in your best interest to verify any information you consume online, lest you become the next in a long line of victims.

What's all the fuss about cyber threats, and where did it all start?

People often think of cyber crimes as something recent, mostly because we come across a lot of information on cyber threats all the time. Well, thanks to widespread internet access and social media, it's easier to come across such information, so I can see why most people think cyber threats are a recent occurrence.

Unfortunately, cyber threats and cybercrime have been around since the early 1940s, right around the time John Mauchly and J. Presper Eckert built the first digital computer, ENIAC, in 1943. Around that time, not many people could afford or knew how to operate the computer system, so cyber threats were practically nonexistent.

While modern cyber threats mostly revolve around data crimes, the earliest threats have nothing to do with data. If anything, people were more interested in making free calls over long distances. This problem started in the 1950s, and lasted around three decades, eating into the profits of phone companies.

For the better part of early computing history, computers were mostly gigantic devices that produced a lot of heat. You'd find them in restricted, controlled environments, therefore, not so many people could access them, and in any case, it would have been so easy to figure out who had access.

What we know today as hacking started in the 1960s, when some individuals gained access to MIT train sets, attempting to alter their functionality. Since computing was still developing, there was no economic gain in having such access. If anything, hacking was purely for the thrill, a bunch of smart or creative folks gaining access and trying to create a scene, either because they can, or to see if it was even possible in the first place.

Come the 1970s, cyber threats had become a real problem. This was the decade when the Advanced Research Projects Agency Network (ARPANET) was built, a networked computer system created specifically for research and academics. One of the ARPANET developers, Bob Thomas, built the first computer worm. It was a rather harmless program that replicated from one device to the next, the Creeper worm. Soon after, Ray Tomlinson, another ARPANET developer, built Reaper, a tool that would search and destroy the Creeper worm.

We can think of the 70s, therefore, as the origin of the first virus and antivirus. By this time, computers were becoming more commonplace, which meant more people had access. The following decade saw a significant increase in breaches, with victims including AT&T and the national CSS. Commercial antivirus programs like Flushot Plus and Anti4us were released in 1987.

The 90s brought most of the world online, and with it, lots of cyber security concerns. From the 2000s onwards, everyone got crazy about the internet. Everything went online, from schools to libraries and transportation systems. The digital landscape has grown so much that without an online presence, you can barely get an audience from some quarters. For example, these days if you're looking for a job, the first thing a prospective employer will do is try to find your professional account on LinkedIn.

Sadly, as the world gets accustomed to the widely evolving digital landscape, the threats keep coming and they get more complicated over time. The online criminal enterprise is so vast and diverse that it is the backdrop against which the dark web (a section of the internet that you cannot access through Google and other everyday search engines) thrives, a very dangerous part of the internet that any ordinary user should never even think of exploring.

Brief History of How the Internet Began

Having briefly outlined the concept of cyber threats, it's clear that without the internet, we probably wouldn't have to worry about such. But then again, given what you know today, and the value of the internet in your life, can you imagine a life without the internet?

It's unthinkable, right?

To protect yourself from online threats, you must learn how they work. I mean, it's almost impossible to protect yourself from something you don't know. Similarly, to understand how online threats work, you must understand how the internet works. But first, a brief history. I mean, everything starts from somewhere, right?

1969 through the 70s

ARPANET was the earliest model of the internet. This model was designed to link four research computers at Stanford Research Institute, UCLA, UCSB, and the University of Utah.

Researchers built on the early success of these four and gradually connected other universities to the research network, whose name would eventually transform into the *Internet*.

Librarians, engineers, researchers, scientists, and computer experts were the earliest target audience for the internet, long before it was adapted for everyday consumers.

The Transport Control Protocol and Internet Protocol (TCP/IP) architecture was also developed in this decade, which made it easier for information and communication transfer. It's against this backdrop that in 1972, emails were introduced.

1980s

This is the decade when the internet evolved from being primarily a research resource to a user-friendly experience, thanks to the National Science Foundation (NSF).

Essentially, NSF installed supercomputers countrywide, as the foundation on which modern computing would thrive. This enabled the evolution of internet use from research and academic purposes to everyday use.

1990s

The University of Minnesota created an interface for users to browse information and research files from various learning institutions that were connected to the internet in 1991. This interface would be later refined and improved by researchers at the University of Nevada (Reno), adding features like indexing and search functions.

NSF stopped sponsoring the NSFNET in 1995 in light of the growing diversity of focus around the evolution of the internet. Since the internet at the time was mostly a research resource, there wasn't any commercial value to it. By discontinuing their support for NSFNET, the NSF essentially paved the way for the commercialization of the internet, creating room for rapid growth and diversity. This is how CompuServe, AOL, Delphi, and Prodigy found their big break, giving birth to the behemoth that is the tech industry we have today.

As the 90s drew to a close, the internet was quite a spectacle. Microsoft's Windows 98, and the debut of wireless networks (WiFi) were crucial aspects in the commercialization of the internet. Essentially, the internet had successfully evolved from research centers in select learning institutions and was now in our homes.

21st Century

What more can we say? You're living through an amazing generation, that's witnessing some of the greatest marvels of the internet. Billions of people all over the world can not only access the internet, but they have it in the palm of their hands.

You've seen it all, from using the internet to vote, to social media, the 21st Century has, and will remain an amazing growth phase for the internet. To be honest, living through this generation feels like anything that can be conceptualized could become a reality.

Think about it for a moment. The Internet is now a crucial infrastructure in collaboration at every possible level. Whether you're talking about collaborating in school, at work, at home, or even at the International Space Station, the Internet is a necessity. This also underpins the statement we made earlier that it's high time we revised the basic human needs and included the internet alongside food, shelter, and clothing.

Here's an interesting stat: Experts believe that by 2030, more than 7 billion people will be able to access the internet from more than 500 billion devices. If you think this is amazing, wait until you explore the prospects of the age of AI that we're currently living through. To quote the famous phrase by Bachman–Turner Overdrive (BTO), You Ain't Seen Nothin' Yet!

How the Internet Works

The internet's history is quite fascinating, almost as fascinating as your browsing history. Now that we have that out of the way, let's explore how the internet works. I mean, what really happens when you use a website?

The answer is quite elaborate, but we'll simplify it in the following 10 steps:

Step 1: Devices and Users

It all starts with individual devices such as computers, smartphones, tablets, and servers, each of which has a unique address known as an Internet Protocol (IP) address. You access the internet through these devices to send and receive data.

Step 2: Data Transmission

When you request a webpage, send an email, or perform any online activity, data is broken down into small packets of information. These packets contain the content you want to transmit, as well as source and destination IP addresses.

Step 3: Local Network

If you're at home or in an office, your device is likely connected to a local network, often through WiFi or Ethernet. Routers manage the local network, routing data between devices within the network and to the internet.

Step 4: Your Internet Service Provider (ISP)

Your local network is connected to the internet through an ISP. ISPs are companies that provide internet connectivity. They have their networks and infrastructure to connect you to the broader internet.

Data from your ISP is transmitted through high-speed, long-distance fiber-optic cables that make up the internet's backbone. These cables span continents and oceans, connecting regions worldwide.

Step 5: Routing

Data packets are passed between routers at various points along their journey. Routers are like traffic cops that decide the most efficient path for data to travel. They use complex algorithms to determine the best route.

Step 6: Servers

When you request a website or an online service, your request is sent to a server. Servers are powerful computers that store and provide access to websites, databases, and other online resources.

Step 7: Domain Name System (DNS)

DNS is like the internet's phonebook. It translates human-readable domain names (e.g., www.google.com) into IP addresses that computers can understand. When you enter a URL, your device queries a DNS server to find the corresponding IP address.

Step 8: Data Exchange

Once your request reaches the appropriate server, it processes the request and sends back data packets to your device. These packets follow the same route in reverse, passing through routers and networks until they reach your ISP and, ultimately, your device.

Step 9: Encryption

Many internet communications are encrypted to protect data from eavesdropping. Secure protocols, like HTTPS for websites, ensure that data is transmitted securely between your device and the server.

Step 10: End User Experience

Your device reassembles the data packets it receives, and you see the requested web page, video, or other content on your screen. This entire process typically happens in milliseconds, making it seem instantaneous to the end user.

Internet Influence on Our Lives

We've constantly mentioned that the internet is a useful resource. To bring this into perspective, let's explore some statistics right after the COVID-19 pandemic that show just how much the internet has transformed our lives.

Communication and Social Interaction

- In 2021, there were approximately 3.96 billion social media users worldwide.
- Over 350 million photos are uploaded to Facebook every day.
- WhatsApp had over 2 billion monthly active users.

Online Shopping

- E-commerce sales reached $4.9 trillion globally in 2021.
- Amazon, one of the largest e-commerce platforms, had over 200 million Prime members in 2021.

Education

- The e-learning market size was estimated to be over $375 billion in 2021.
- The COVID-19 pandemic led to a surge in online education, with over 1.6 billion students affected by school closures.

Work and Remote Employment

- Remote work became more common due to the pandemic, with approximately 42% of the U.S. workforce working from home in 2021.
- Video conferencing platform Zoom reported over 300 million daily meeting participants.

Healthcare

Telemedicine usage surged during the pandemic, with a 154% increase in telehealth visits in the U.S. in 2020.

Thanks to social media, the internet has bridged the gap between communities, truly making the world a global village. It is a platform through which people can express themselves and engage on diverse subjects regardless of their geographical location. It brings people together from all over the world through global events like the World Cup, the Super Bowl, and Tomorrowland, so much so that even without your physical presence, you can still get in on the action.

Given the rapid growth and influence that the internet has in our lives, it's clear to see why cyber threats exist, as criminal entities try to take advantage of this growth and exert their nefarious activities on individuals and society in general.

A Brief History of Cybercrime

The National Institute of Standards and Technology (NIST) defines cyber threats as events or circumstances posing adverse risks to individuals, organizational operations, and assets by way of unauthorized access to an information system. Such events usually involve denial of service, disclosure, destruction, or malicious modification of data. NIST also classifies the successful exploitation of known or unknown vulnerabilities in an information system as cyber threats, especially when this exploit is from persons or organizations with illegitimate access to the information systems.

Having explored a brief overview of the evolution of cyber threats from the 1940s earlier in the book, let's take a moment and look at some of the prominent exploits over the years. Cybercrime has evolved over the years, so much that it's now recognized as an independent, yet illegitimate industry worth more than $1.5 trillion. Thus, we can't list all the hacks, but we can point out a few that grabbed the headlines:

1962 - Allen Scherr uses a punch card to steal passwords from MIT computer networks

1971 - Bob Thomas creates the first computer virus, the Creeper Virus

1988 - Robert Morris executes the first seismic cyber attack. Using the Morris Worm, he infected computer networks at major academic research institutions, including Princeton, Stanford, NASA, and John Hopkins.

1994 - 16-year-old schoolboys use password sniffers to exploit The Air Force's Rome Labs, getting away with some battle instructions.

1995 - Vladimir Levin hacked Citibank's network, stealing over $10 million

1999 - The Melissa Virus strikes, compromising users across the globe by targeting Microsoft suite files.

2000 - 15-year-old Mafiaboy (Michael Calse) executes DDoS exploits on prominent websites like eBay, CNN, Yahoo, and Amazon, costing the sites millions of dollars by simply being inaccessible for a few hours.

2008 - Heartland Payment Systems is breached, exposing data for more than 130 million users.

2010 - Iranian nuclear plants are attacked by the Stuxnet worm, crippling their uranium enrichment systems.

2010 - American banks lose more than $70 million to the Zeus trojan virus

2010 - China executes Operation Aurora, targeting top tech companies, with Google reporting the seizure of their intellectual property.

2011 - Sony Corporation's PlayStation network is compromised, exposing privileged information for more than 77 million users. It would take Sony over three weeks to fix the problem.

2013 - Edward Snowden blows the whistle on the National Security Agency's (NSA) surveillance program, PRISM, that spied and stole privileged information from foreign government agents.

2013 - A phishing exploit on Target sees credit card information for more than 100 million customers stolen.

2015 - The Pentagon takes down its email system in response to a phishing attack targeting the Defense Department. The breach exposed the records of thousands of civilian and military personnel.

2017 - The WannaCry ransomware exploits hundreds of thousands of computers across 150 countries. A few weeks later, NotPetya, an update to WannaCry, is executed to devastating effect.

2018 - An elaborate DDoS attack cripples GitHub, flooding traffic at 1.3 terabytes a second.

2019 - Capital One spends $150 million in damage mitigation in the wake of a breach that exposed more than 100 million credit card records.

2020 - Russian operatives commandeer the SolarWinds program, exploiting thousands of U.S. government institutions and making away with source code, personal, and financial information.

2021 - The Colonial Pipeline is taken offline by Russian hackers, disrupting the supply of diesel, gasoline, and jet fuel mostly to the East Coast.

2022 - Ride-share company Uber is hacked, giving the hackers full access to the company's inner sanctum, including code repositories, cloud storage facilities, internal memos, communications, and privileged emails.

We've barely scratched the surface if we were to explore the full spectrum of notable hacks, but you can see the sheer magnitude of the damage that cyberattacks can cause. For example, did you know that at the time of the 2021 hack, Colonial Pipeline was responsible for close to 50% of the fuel needs of the East Coast? Thus, you can only imagine the kind of crisis the East Coast was plunged into, with shortages, hoarding, and price hikes.

Sophistication and efficiency are evident in the history of the internet, just in the same way as they are in the history of cybercrime. It's important to note that as the internet evolves, so does cybercrime. Criminals get craftier by the day, and this isn't helped by the fact that most elaborate criminal syndicates invest in some of the best technologies out there, to support their criminal agenda.

The fact that both good and evil exist on the internet isn't a surprise, as this is just a normal phenomenon in our society. Therefore, although the internet is an important resource that plays an important role in the advancement of humanity, there will always be criminal elements looking to exploit this for nefarious reasons. As we mentioned earlier, your goal is to try and make sure you never fall victim to such elements, and this book will show you how.

Finally, we come online to seek information. In this age of fake news and AI-generated material, it's not always easy to know who's telling the truth and who's lying. When it comes to cybersecurity, it's even more important that you know where to get authentic information. With that in mind, here's a list of institutes and agencies from which you can seek authentic information on cybersecurity.

- Center for Internet Security (CIS) (https://www. cisecurity.org/)
- Cloud Security Alliance (CSA) (https:// cloudsecurityalliance.org/)
- National Institute of Standards and Technology (NIST) (https://www.nist.gov/)
- National Cyber Security Alliance (https:// staysafeonline.org/)
- SANS Institute (https://www.sans.org/apac/)
- Cybersecurity and Infrastructure Security Agency (CISA) (https://www.cisa.gov/)

Apart from their oversight on security matters, you can also access them as useful resources to expand your knowledge on cybersecurity.

Building on this knowledge, let's now take an exploratory dive into the psychology of hackers, to help us gain insight into their intricate motivations, and use this to understand the multifaceted world of cybersecurity.

2

Inside the Psyche of Hackers and Cybercriminals

H ave you ever been scammed online?

It's quite an unsettling experience, one that you wouldn't wish on anyone. If you've had the misfortune of falling victim to cyber criminals, then you probably understand the mental torment that comes after.

Why would someone do that to me?

How would someone just wake up one morning and decide to take advantage of me, a stranger, who has done them no harm at all?

Are some people just evil?

Here's an interesting fact—a hacker's decision to take advantage of you probably had nothing to do with you in the first place. You're just a victim who happened to fall into their trap. To help you avoid such incidents in the future, let's explore what goes on in the minds of cybercriminals. They say set a thief to catch a thief, right? By understanding a hacker's motives, it's easier to get a better insight into the world of cybercrime, and from that knowledge, you'll be well-equipped to protect yourself and avoid scams. At the end of the day, cybercrime, like most criminal events, is purely a psychological exploit. By the time a criminal lures you in and steals from you, they will have already beaten you in a psychological game that you might not even have been aware of in the first place.

Hackers will exploit you from miles away, at times, even continents apart. It's unfathomable, because most of the time, you'd assume that someone close to you leaked your information online, but that's not usually the case. Since hackers cannot find you physically, the best they can do is set intricate traps to lure you in, and all this from behind a screen. Instead of coming to you, they reel you in and bring you to them.

One thing you'll need to know about hackers is that they are just human like each one of us. For that reason, you can avoid being a pawn in their game by learning the drive and purpose behind their actions. That's how you protect yourself.

There are two different kinds of hackers, black hat and white hat. Interestingly enough, the path to hacking for each of these hackers starts the same way. A hacker generally develops a passion and interest in tech fields like scripting, visualization, networking, and programming. As this interest evolves, they assume different paths. While white hat hackers use their skill, talent, and passion to solve problems, black hat hackers create problems.

While both hackers generally have the same set of skills, the biggest difference between them is their motivation. Black hat hackers are dangerous and mostly engage in illegal activities. Black hat hackers are malicious and will take advantage of the slightest opportunity to exploit you, usually for personal gain.

On the other hand, white hat hackers are ethical hackers who generally use their talent and skills to make the digital world a better place. Companies hire white hat hackers to help them find weaknesses in their systems and create solutions to protect their interests and those of their customers.

Apart from their inherent skills, most hackers are also driven by their personality traits. If someone is generally a bad person, possessing hacking skills makes them a threat, since they'll probably use their skills for illegal or bad deeds. On the other hand, if someone is a good person, there's a higher chance that they'll use their skills to perpetuate good fortune in society. These, unfortunately, are not necessarily cast in stone. There have been good people who ended up being black hat hackers for various reasons, and other bad people who became ethical hackers. At the end of the day, a hacker's destiny comes down to the choices they make, and the circumstances unfolding in their lives.

Here are some possible reasons why black hat hackers target unsuspecting victims online:

- The thrill - Even though most criminal hackers do it for money, some of them do it for the adrenaline rush, just to prove that they can do it. It's more of an ego boost for them, trying to breach systems that are otherwise presented as impenetrable.
- Creative genius - You can't just get up one day and hack a system. You must be meticulous and methodical in your approach. This calls for creativity, and in some cases, a stroke of genius. Hackers have to think outside the box to identify and exploit vulnerabilities.
- Knowledge - Hackers take time to understand how systems work. They study different systems, their code structure, strengths, and vulnerabilities.

- Criminal minds - Well, most hacking is illegal. You're essentially trying to gain access to privileged information, for your own nefarious reasons.

The Cybercrime Triangle

As the world of tech evolves, so does the global criminal enterprise. As we mentioned earlier, criminals invest in the latest tech just as much as you do, and some of them invest even more than you do. The core of this book is to show you how to thwart the efforts of a determined criminal. In this section, we'll borrow a leaf from an approach that firefighters use all the time, the fire triangle.

A fire triangle supposes that three things must be present for any fire to exist:

- A source of fuel
- Oxygen
- Heat

In the presence of these three, a fire will not just start, but it will also sustain itself, causing further damage along the way. Thus, all you have to do to prevent, contain, or stop a fire, is to eliminate at least one of the three.

Now, cybercrime works in the same way. Let's explore the three crucial factors that must be present for every criminal activity, and what you can do about them below:

- **The Opportunity**

These are the vulnerabilities in your system. To be honest, even the most robust security system has flaws, and in most cases, the weakest link is usually the human element or interface. Understand your vulnerabilities and constantly work towards limiting your exposure. Bring in auditors, and other security experts from time to time to review your systems to build robust and resilient security architecture around the things you hold dear.

- **The Criminal**

These are the bad actors around you. Unfortunately, there are far too many criminals around for you to accurately predict when they'll attack or where they'll attack from. At times, the threat emanates from within your organization, either knowingly or not, and in some cases, the threat is external. The threat could also come from your immediate competitors or a disgruntled customer.

The smartest approach to handling threats is to create an elaborate mitigation policy and ensure everyone knows about it, and the appropriate steps to take in the event of a breach. Engage law enforcement at every step of the way. Most entities try to sweep their vulnerability exploits under the rug to save face. Unfortunately, such information still leaks at some point. Be proactive and engage authorities when you've been attacked, so they can follow up and handle it to the full extent of the law.

- **The Victim**

You're the target. Everything comes down to how you handle yourself online. What information do you share online, and with whom? What steps have you taken to protect your online accounts? What third-party programs are you using, and what privileges have you granted them on your devices?

More often, criminals come across potential victims without even making an effort because we're careless with our information and online activity. For example, we're always advised not to use public Wi-Fi, yet you'll still find a lot of people crowded around a local hotspot, oblivious of the risks they're exposing themselves to.

Be vigilant. After all, you are your first line of defense!

The biggest lesson from our cybercrime triangle is that if you're going to protect yourself, you have to think bigger. Don't just think about what criminals can or will do to you, but make yourself part of the solution. Think about what you can do in whichever capacity, to create a robust environment that deters criminals. As they say, prevention is better than cure. In the case of cybercrime, prevention means being able to preempt criminal intent and taking proactive measures to stop them in their tracks.

To sum this up, cybercrime is all around us. Never overestimate the strength of the security measures you have in place. At the same time, never underestimate the potential threat risk of a determined criminal. Do your best to limit your organization's exposure as much as possible. In the event of a breach or a suspicious attempt on your organization, do not sit on it. Report to the relevant authorities and provide as much information as possible. You never know, your report might just flag something bigger than your organization.

Note that the concept above applies to all criminal activities, not just cybercrime. My hope, therefore, is that you can apply this knowledge in other areas of your life too, and boost security around your home, your office, and anything else that might be valuable to you.

The Cyberpsychology of Bad Actors

Given our knowledge of the cybercrime triangle, the next question we should be asking ourselves is what motivates criminals to come after you? If you can get clarity on this, then it's easier to work on your security systems and be prepared for whichever threats might come your way.

From my experience in the industry, the solution lies in the question, what does the criminal stand to gain from all this? Your systems could be targeted for any of the following three reasons:

- **Criminal Motivations**

The motive behind such attacks is usually financial. The aim could be to disrupt your business, steal and sell your data, or simply steal your money. Such criminals could either scout your system through different social engineering tactics where you'll unknowingly usher them into your security architecture through the front door.

There's a thriving market for user data on the dark web, so such criminals could either sell your data, extort you for ransom, or both. Since most individual victims usually can't afford the ransom, most of these criminals target companies, knowing that they have more to lose in case their data falls in the wrong hands.

Your competitors or someone who holds a grudge against your business could also try to breach your security framework to access privileged information that could give them an edge over you in the industry. We also have vigilante hackers, with a vendetta against your business, who exploit your vulnerabilities and air your dirty linen in public. Essentially, they aim to create fear among your customers, deterring them from doing business with you.

- **Personal Motivations**

A personally motivated hacker is just as dangerous as the criminal elements we discussed above. You can never truly tell the depth of their vendetta, because it could be driven by anything from a grudge, curiosity, or perhaps they're just hoping to get recognized in the criminal world. It gets worse because some of these could be former employees or just someone unhappy with their job, so they already have a way into your security apparatus.

- **Political Motivations**

You could also fall victim to hackers for political reasons. This can be unfortunate because you might not even have any interest in the subject of their hacktivism, yet someone was motivated enough to come after you. More often, such hackers target critical architecture or anything that could support their agenda. In some cases, hacktivists don't necessarily wish to, or aim to cause widespread damage to their victims, but to raise their profile, or drive attention towards their cause.

Living in the age of digital warfare, we've also seen instances where countries sponsor attacks against their enemies. For example, in the ongoing war between Russia and Ukraine, both countries have had critical infrastructure being targeted by hackers. Unfortunately, in such wars, the hackers could be from any country in the world, and might not necessarily be directly or indirectly motivated by the Russia-Ukraine war.

Cyber Criminals and Social Engineering

Most people generally refer to cyber criminals as hackers. While all cyber criminals could be hackers, not all hackers are cybercriminals. A hacker is someone who has some technical computer skills. What determines whether a hacker is good or bad is how they use their skills.

There are hackers whose work is for the greater good and mostly work within the confines of the law. We call them white hat hackers. Such hackers can be tasked with penetration testing, which helps to identify vulnerabilities in a system, report them to developers, and have them create appropriate fixes.

We also have black hat hackers. These are criminals, who use their tech skills without any regard for the law and are always pursuing malicious intent. Between black hat and white hat hackers, we have the grey hat hackers. Grey hat hackers may violate ethical and legal standards from time to time, but they are generally not motivated by the deeply rooted malice of black hat hackers.

Hackers can also work under an organized framework, with clear instructions, targets, and goals. Such hackers are well-remunerated and generally use their skills for a cause they believe in. They include state-sponsored hackers, terrorists, and hacktivists.

Other kinds of cyber criminals you might come across include the following:

- Identity thieves - They steal your information and can create a new digital identity which they can use for any number of reasons.
- Cyberstalkers - They are like every other stalker you might come across offline. They follow your every move online and gather as much information as possible through malware or social media, to harass you. Cyberstalkers can also come after identifiable groups or organizations.
- Phishing scammers - These criminals have perfected the art of social engineering, and can easily lure you into giving them your personal information, installing malware on your devices, or whatever other reason behind their actions.
- Disgruntled employees - An unhappy employee is a dangerous employee, especially when they have access to privileged resources, like admin credentials, or physical access to your server room. Gone are the days when employees would go on strike, or issue a go-slow. While that still happens, it's easier to box employers into a corner by initiating a malicious hack.

Most criminal activities online happen because the hacker manages to convince you to do something, or to trust them. They cultivate a false element of trust, and with that, you let them in. Trust is at the center of social engineering, and this is how criminals persuade you to share sensitive information with them, or at times, they subtly guide you into making a costly mistake.

You don't just happen to be a victim of social engineering. If anything, very few exploits are random. More often, criminals put a lot of effort into making this work. To be precise, it's a four-phase process that's executed as follows:

- **Phase 1 - Investigation**

This is the planning phase, where hackers identify potential victims or targets with lucrative payoffs. The kind of target they come after and their intended payoffs determine the strategies they'll execute to rope you in.

- **Phase 2 - Baiting**

This is where they cultivate the false sense of trust that will compromise you. It could be anything that plays to your interests or weaknesses. Remember, they've already researched you so they know a bit about you, your browsing habits, websites you frequent, and so on. They set the bait, for example, with a story you'll probably believe, a download link to a file you need, or a link to a website you frequent.

- **Phase 3 - Attack**

At this point, your devices are compromised, and the criminals have infiltrated your digital empire. This is where they carry out their plan. They'll steal your data, disrupt your network, change your system settings, create a backdoor they can use whenever they need to, and so on. Once they are in, it's impossible to tell the true extent of the damage, or whether they have a short-term or long-term agenda.

- **Phase 4 - Adios!**

Their mission is complete, so they sneak out of your system and network. Some criminals will exit the scene stealthily, without leaving a trail. In this case, there's a good chance they have a backdoor already and will come and go as they please because you'll never realize they were there in the first place. Other criminals create so much havoc, you'll rue the day you fell for their tricks.

If you ever fall victim to a social engineering exploit, don't beat yourself up. Use it as a learning experience and be bolder and more careful next time. Remember, social engineering isn't just about randomly coming across a victim and taking advantage of them. There's a science to it, an elaborate psychological game you might not even realize you're in. At times, criminals use the strategies legitimate market companies use. For example, marketers use a false sense of scarcity to cultivate an element of urgency. You'll act fast so you don't miss out on a hot deal when in the real sense, there was no deal. The price might even be higher than it's supposed to be, but since you don't want to miss out on the "deal", you do everything possible to get it.

It's mostly a game of psychological manipulation that appeals to your desires. They target your weaknesses, sometimes try to gain favor or be likable, and in some cases, they instill fear in you. Once they have a target and are certain the payoffs will be lucrative, criminals are consistent. They'll hammer in the message at every chance they get, chipping away at your psychological defenses gradually until you give in and usher them in through the front gate.

You can't always successfully identify and fend off potential attacks, but if you're vigilant, you can protect yourself against most social engineering attacks. The pattern for most of these attacks is quite simple, grammatical errors, typos, ridiculous language constructs, persuasion, or threats. Don't be quick to act on their call to action. Spare a few minutes to investigate before making a move. The FBI runs the Internet Crime Complaint Center (IC3), a centralized platform where you can learn more about cyber attacks as they evolve, and also report attacks for further investigation. Check it out sometime.

Interactive Element

Q1. What motivates cybercriminals to engage in illegal activities?

Cybercriminals are often driven by financial gain, seeking ways to profit through illicit means such as stealing personal information, financial data, or intellectual property. Some are also motivated by ideological reasons, seeking to disrupt systems for political or social reasons.

Q2. How do cybercriminals typically approach their targets?

Cybercriminals employ various tactics like phishing, malware, or social engineering to exploit vulnerabilities in systems or manipulate individuals. They exploit cybersecurity weaknesses to gain unauthorized access to networks, devices, or sensitive data.

Q3. What guides the actions of cybercriminals?

Unlike ethical hackers, cybercriminals operate outside legal and ethical boundaries. Their actions often disregard laws, morals, and the potential harm caused to individuals or organizations. Their primary focus is on achieving their objectives, often at the expense of others' security and privacy.

In the realm of cybersecurity, the motivations and methodologies used by hackers are pivotal in comprehending the ever-changing threat landscape. Every hacker has an agenda, and it could be anything from curiosity-driven exploration to profit-seeking and geopolitical agendas. These ultimately set the stage for the never-ending pursuit of vulnerabilities to be exploited across networks and devices. In the next chapter, we dive into the end product of a hacker's mindset, the modern threats we are exposed to every other day.

3

Modern Cyber Threats: The Complete List from A-Z

One of the best things about the internet is that it can be anything you want it to be. Sadly, that's also one of the worst things about it. The internet could be your school, your escape from boredom, an opportunity to explore and push your creative limits, and so on. On the flip side, it can also be the beginning of the end for you, if you happen to cross paths with cybercriminals. Most people only know of common infections like a computer virus, ransomware, or spam. While these can be severe, they barely scratch the surface of the potential risks you face online. There are more threats out there than most online users can begin to understand.

The internet is a resource, a useful one to be precise. The thing about resources is that everyone finds a way to make the most use of them. While you, for example, might use the internet to improve or enhance different aspects of your life, criminals share the same sentiments. The only difference is that their improvement and enhancement come at your expense.

There are more cyber threats today than there were yesterday, and the number increases exponentially with each passing day. This means that each time you come online, you're always exposed to the risk of an attack. Whether the attack is successful or not, will depend on the measures you have in place. Knowledge of the potential risks can go a long way, helping you protect your online activity, both at work and at home.

Awareness is not a one-time thing. It's an ongoing learning process that will help you know not only the potential risks you face online, but also how to prevent them, and what to do in the unfortunate event of an attack. Remember that the threats keep evolving, and become more severe. This is why it's important to learn about the possible threats and effective management techniques.

To help you stay vigilant and protect your digital lifestyle, the section below details a complete list of modern cyber threats you should be aware of.

Denial-of-Service (DoS) Attack

As the name suggests, this attack simply floods your network with more traffic than it can handle, impeding its ability to hold its own, and effectively crippling your operations. When hackers deploy multiple devices to execute this attack, it becomes a distributed denial of service attack (DDoS). Here are some examples of a DoS attack:

- **HTTP Flood DDoS**

In this approach, the hacker overwhelms your system by sending HTTP requests that would appear to be normal, only that they are not. Your system will struggle by trying to assign the limited resources available to each request, effectively interrupting your service.

- **ICMP Flood**

Your system will struggle due to the overwhelming inbound and outbound bandwidth demand coming from ICMP echo request packets submitted by hackers, slowing down in the long run, or collapsing altogether.

- **NTP Amplification**

The fact that network time protocol (NTP) servers are accessible to the public makes them vulnerable, and easily accessible to hackers. All they have to do is push more traffic to a network than it is built to handle. This is how most DDoS attacks are executed.

Injection Attacks

These attacks generally exploit existing vulnerabilities in program code, allowing hackers control over the programs for their intended objectives. Once hackers identify a weakness in your program code, they can push their code in alongside yours, which the program will interpret and continue to run as legitimate commands. Unfortunately, while you might not realize it, the injected code will instruct the program to operate contrary to its original blueprint. Examples of such attacks include the following:

- Code injection
- Cross-Site Scripting (XSS)
- LDAP injection
- OS command injection
- SQL injection
- XML eXternal Entities (XXE) Injection

These attacks can be used for anything from compromising your entire system, stealing user credentials, and information, or even executing a DDoS attack.

Malware Attacks

Malware is one of the most common forms of attack, malicious software that can collect data from your devices, block network access, or even destroy your data and in some cases, shut down your system. You might even end up with a persistent shut-down loop, where your device boots and shuts down instantly. Malware includes the following:

• **Adware**

These are usually loaded in ads, and their purpose is to monitor and record your online activity. Advertisers use information about your browsing behavior to push targeted ads or ads that appeal to your immediate needs. For example, if you're constantly visiting car-related websites, you'll start seeing more ads about cars, car parts, upholstery, accessories, and so on.

While adware generally doesn't install malicious software on your devices, some criminals have used adware for that very reason. Besides, the fact that adware can be used without your consent puts a heavy price on your privacy.

- **Cryptojacking**

Crypto mining is a big business, and miners reap great benefits in the process. However, mining is quite a resource-intensive process, and some crafty miners can "outsource" some of the required computing power from unsuspecting users.

Cryptojacking is a situation where someone stealthily installs mining software on your computer. You'll probably notice your computer getting slower over time, but you can't figure out why. You might even think the hardware is obsolete and upgrade your processing power, much to the hacker's advantage.

- **Fileless Malware**

Instead of installing malicious programs on your computer, the criminals will simply edit important files and functions like PowerShell to serve their needs. Ideally, the edited files are not infected, but they are not performing the tasks that they were meant to, or even if they are, not as efficiently as they were designed to. This is one of the reasons why this kind of attack is not easy to detect. It's like using a spoon instead of a fork. At the end of the day, you're still eating, right?

- **Ransomware**

This is like a typical hostage situation, where kidnappers ask for some money before they can release your loved ones. Similarly, hackers exploit and take over your devices, locking you out until you pay a ransom. Unfortunately, there's never a guarantee that the hackers will allow you full or any access at all to your devices once you pay the ransom, so it's quite a tricky situation.

- **Rootkits**

Rootkits are software that give hackers administrative rights over your devices, or even your entire network. Once they have administrator access, there's no limit to what they can do, including installing more stealthy malware, just in case you figure the rootkit out and wipe it clean.

- **Spyware**

Spyware can be installed through your mobile phone apps, desktop apps, browsers, and anything else you use on your devices. As the name suggests, spyware is mostly about information gathering. Most criminals are interested in your payment details and access credentials, even though spyware could also be used to monitor your activity, for example, if you're working on a lucrative but secret project.

- **Trojans**

You'll never notice trojans because they are often camouflaged as or in legitimate programs. If you download and use pirated software, you've probably installed a lot of trojans on your devices, because they are commonly fronted as license key generators. Once the trojan is activated in your system, hackers have full access and can deploy any kind of attack.

- **Viruses**

A virus is simply a malicious piece of code written into an application, that executes each time you run that application. For example, if someone loads a virus on your Microsoft Office Suite, the virus runs each time you run any of the components of the suite, for example, Excel, Word, or PowerPoint.

- **Worms**

Worms exploit weaknesses in your system and kill you from within. For example, hackers could identify a manufacturer-level system flaw on one of the devices on your IoT network, and use it to gain access to your computer. Once they are in, they could easily deploy a DDoS attack, cutting you off from your business.

Man-in-the-Middle Attack

Man-in-the-middle (MitM) attacks exploit the vacuum of trust that exists between two entities. Hackers identify their victims and position themselves in the middle of their engagement, intercepting their communication. In some cases, the hacker could even maliciously alter the message to suit their intentions, without either party realizing they have been compromised. Hackers could even impersonate either party and take over the entire conversation, leaving the other party in the dark, unaware that the engagement might still be going on.

Here are some examples of such attacks:

- **DNS Spoofing**

In this case, hackers spoof the domain name server (DNS) redirecting you to a fake website, but since you're oblivious to this, you'll engage the fake website as if you were using the legitimate site, allowing them to steal your data.

- **Email Hijacking**

Hackers clone email addresses from legitimate entities, like your insurer, your bank, or even e-commerce platforms like Amazon and eBay. With the new email address, they engage you and request personal information. Some hackers can even give you instructions to transfer money from your account to theirs.

- **HTTPS Spoofing**

HTTPS as a security standard is a fact that we'll mention throughout this book. However, criminals are also aware of this. So since they know that most potential victims will shy away from an HTTP website, they create fake websites but implement the HTTPS security standard. Most people let their guard down once they notice HTTPS, and that's how criminals get away with whatever they came for.

- **IP Spoofing**

This concept is similar to all the others we've discussed above. The hacker simply clones a legitimate IP address, and fools you into believing that you are engaging a legitimate website when in the real sense, you're operating in a circus of their making.

- **Wi-Fi Eavesdropping**

This is a more intrusive approach because hackers set up an entity that you can trust. For example, they could create a wireless network that serves an area whose residents they wish to exploit. They'd then sell the wireless service to business and home users, and use that opportunity to monitor all the traffic that flows through their network and extract valuable information from them. This is also one of the reasons why you're usually advised against using free Wi-Fi hotspots because you never know whose network it is, or their intentions.

Social Engineering Attacks

Social engineering represents the tactics hackers use to manipulate or coerce you into giving them information you normally wouldn't share with anyone. You could also be duped into visiting websites or platforms you wouldn't, downloading programs you have no business using in the first place, sending the criminals money, or engaging in activities that you generally don't. The whole point of social engineering is to compromise your security in some capacity, but the fallback will always track back to you. The criminals make it appear as if you did it all willingly, and are fully aware of your actions, especially since they often present themselves as a legitimate entity. Here are examples of social engineering attacks:

- **Baiting**

This works in the same way you bait your catch when you go fishing. Fish like worms, so you attach one on a hook and wait for a bite. Hackers lure you with something you'll be interested in, for example, the promise of a gift card, coupons, or anything else. Once you click on the link, you fill out a form giving them your credentials, and signing up to fake platforms, but the gift card or whatever you were promised may never come.

- **Clickjacking Attack**

Criminals execute this attack by creating a decoy user interface, and that's why it's also known as a US redress attack. In this case, criminals create and hide behind multiple layers to trick you into clicking something on a website. Unknown to you, the website you're visiting is a decoy. For example, you might think you're using website A, but in the real sense, you're using the criminal's website, hidden behind several layers you might not realize. Each click on the decoy website results in an actionable click on the criminal's website. You might think you're opening a new tab, but in the real sense, you've downloaded malware from the criminal's website.

- **Pharming Attack**

This is an elaborate form of phishing that involves two steps. First, hackers find a way to install malicious code into your system. Once the code is installed, it redirects you to the hacker's spooked website, where the hacker will steal your information. It's more or less a clickjacking attack.

- **Phishing**

In this case, hackers send you emails pretending to be someone else. For example, you could receive an email that seems to come from Amazon, but in the real sense, it's not. Unfortunately, you might engage the content in this email assuming you're interacting with an Amazon representative, and share sensitive information with them.

- **Piggybacking**

This kind of attack involves someone pretending to have lost or misplaced their credentials, and "innocently" asks to use yours.

For example, a criminal could pose as a new employee, and approach you during one of the busiest times of your day, or a time when they are certain that no one else will be available to assist, so you'll have no option but to come through for them. The "new employee" asks you to sign them in using your credentials because, for some reason, they cannot use theirs, and just like that, they'll execute a crime, but the audit trail will only lead back to you.

- **Pretexting**

This follows a similar pattern to baiting, only that the criminal pressures you into revealing the information they need, instead of baiting you gently with something you desire. They generally compel you into compliance by pretending to be authority figures in society, for example, an IRS agent, an attorney, a municipal inspection officer, or even a police officer.

- **Smishing (SMS Phishing)**

This is a typical phishing attack, only that it's executed via SMS messaging. The hacker sends you a deceptive message, hoping to convince you to share some information with them, download and install malicious applications or programs, or redirect you to dangerous links where your information will be stolen.

Common examples include the outrageous Nigerian Prince scams, the fake raffle scam, password reset scam, where your email address is already compromised, and since they don't have the two-factor authentication code, they ask you to send it to them.

- **Tailgating**

This is where a criminal trails you to gain physical access to an unauthorized facility or location. They'll even walk in with you but will deceive you into signing them in. Unfortunately, you're never that they're using you until it's too late and they've made away with whatever they came to steal.

- **Vishing (Voice Phishing)**

This kind of attack usually targets the vulnerable in society, for example, the elderly. The criminal simply engages the victim over the phone, posing as someone they can trust, and extracts some useful information from them.

While this kind of attack mostly targets the elderly, it can be carefully orchestrated based on the information hackers have and used on anyone. For example, if you have school-going kids and you are at work, a criminal could simply call and pretend to be one of your children's classmates.

- **Watering Hole Attack**

Animals always gather at a common watering hole to quench their thirst. That's the concept criminals implement with this exploit. It is a targeted attack aimed at a specific group of people, a business, or an industry, who use a common website (the watering hole). For example, if criminals want to target car importers and exporters, they could compromise a website like sbtjapan.com which their target audience visits frequently. From there, they lure you to their landing page, loaded with malware or any other kind of infection to execute their intended attack.

Supply Chain Attacks

Criminals understand that it's not easy to penetrate some of their biggest targets directly, so instead of wasting their effort on a company like HP directly, for example, they go after trusted third parties in their supply chain. Once they exploit the third parties, they gain easy entry into their main target and their customers.

Supply chain attacks could be executed at both hardware and software levels, causing untold suffering to all those who interact with the main target's products. In 2013, for example, hackers exploited an HVAC contractor, and used their access to Target, something they might not have been able to do if they approached Target directly.

Such attacks pose a significant risk today, especially since most businesses do not build their code from scratch. Many entities are building businesses off software vendors, open-source code, and third-party APIs, so there's a lot of room for exposure. To be precise, most software projects today use dependencies from multiple, even hundreds of sources. The entire project is at risk if any of these are compromised.

The biggest challenge in supply chain attacks is the level of trust that the targeted entity has in the certified vendors. As long as the vendor remains unaware that they might have been compromised, the hacker's code will run uninterrupted, with admin-level privileges.

Other Attacks

The attack clusters we've discussed above don't cover everything you need to know about cyberattacks. This is a vastly evolving field, so you can be certain that hackers keep seeking out vulnerabilities they could exploit in your systems all the time.

A password attack, for example, is where hackers use different techniques to sniff your network and steal your password. Once they have these credentials, they can use them to execute any of the attacks we mentioned earlier.

We also have the threat of actors like terrorists, state-sponsored attacks, industry-competitor attacks, acts of hacktivists, actions of malicious insiders, and most recently, with the prevalence of AI, hackers could engineer an AI-orchestrated attack on your network. Others are as follows:

- **Advanced persistent threat (APT)**

This is a stealthy approach, where hackers gain access to your network or devices, and stay undetected for a very long time. APT attacks are targeted and specific and are mostly for surveillance purposes, hence the hackers' need for a stealthy approach. Once they are in your system, they'll learn all they need to know about you, and from there, you could be vulnerable to data theft, interrupting your workflow, or destruction.

- **Brute Force Attack**

This is a trial-and-error method that criminals use to guess, and in many cases, crack your passwords. It can also give them access to your encryption keys and other login credentials. As you'd imagine, anyone who tries to guess your credentials will first try obvious possibilities like your name, year of birth, pets, names of your kids, and so on. Brute force attacks are quite reliable, so don't write it off because of the trial and error concept.

- **Insider Threat**

These are malicious actions by someone on the inside. It could be a disgruntled employee, someone spying for a competitor, or at times, even an innocent mistake. Anyone who has privileged access to your systems can always be a threat. That's why they say the human element is one of the weakest points in any secure system.

- **Keylogger Attack**

Many employers use keyloggers to track what their employees do on their computers all day. While it's an intrusive approach, it's also one of the easiest ways for employers to keep an audit trail of user engagements during work hours, and also to assess productivity.

Unfortunately, criminals also use the same tactic, but in their case, they monitor your keystrokes as you type, to collect user credentials and any other information that might be useful to their nefarious agenda. Hackers load keyloggers into your system through cloud programs, downloaded files, emails, or even infected software.

- **Session Hijacking Attack**

This is a type of hack where criminals simply take over your active online session, giving them access to your data and other relevant information like your browsing history.

- **Zero-day Exploit**

This is a situation where hackers become aware of a software vulnerability before anyone else does, not even the software developers or antivirus developers. They use this opportunity to attack before anyone figures out the problem and creates a solution. This is why it's usually advisable to wait a few weeks before you install the latest version of a program. Early adopters usually take the biggest hit.

The severity of each of the attacks above is relative to the hacker's objectives. Some hackers obtain privileged information to sell on the black market, while others obtain information to execute an even bigger attack. The difficulty level will also come down to an assessment of the loss, and the potential damage if that information falls into the wrong hands.

Luckily, most of the cyber threats we've discussed can be preempted and prevented through a robust security apparatus. At times, it's the simple things like installing and updating your antivirus and training your team on basic security measures that make the biggest difference in protecting your digital ecosystem.

Whether you are running a business or trying to protect your home network, your ability to procure a robust and resilient security architecture might be limited by your finances. However, you cannot afford to not try. When it comes to cybersecurity, you're better off having even the most basic solutions than none at all.

When it comes to cybersecurity, there's never an end to what you can learn. That's why entities like the Cybersecurity & Infrastructure Security Agency (CISA) exist.

Interactive Element

Q1. What can you do to protect yourself from social engineering attacks?

Being cautious and skeptical is key. Always verify the identity of the person you're communicating with, avoid sharing sensitive information over unsolicited emails or calls, and undergo regular cybersecurity awareness training to know how to recognize and handle potential threats.

Q2. How can cyber threats interfere with your life or business?

Modern cyber threats pose significant risks at both individual and corporate levels. They can result in financial losses, and data breaches leading to the exposure of sensitive information, disruption of operations, damage to reputation, and even potential legal consequences.

Q3. What strategies can help mitigate these cyber threats?

You must implement a multi-layered approach. This includes regular software updates and patches, implementing robust cybersecurity measures such as firewalls and encryption, conducting employee training on recognizing and responding to threats (like phishing emails) and establishing incident response plans to swiftly address and contain any breaches. Additionally, employing the principle of least privilege and regularly backing up data can help reduce the impact of cyber attacks.

Given what you now know about the threats you face online all the time, your privacy and security should take precedence at all times. How do you stay safe online? How do you protect your home network from intrusion? What measures can you take to strengthen your security? Well, we answer these and other questions in the next chapter.

PART II

Defense Across All Dimensions Of Your Digital Life

"Against those skilled in attack, an enemy does not know where to defend; against the experts in defense, the enemy does not know where to attack."

Sun Tzu

4

The Privacy Paradox: Balancing Digital Identity and Personal Security

S ome people say online privacy is a myth. This is quite a bold statement, and you could successfully argue for, against, or support both arguments with valid resources. But, away from the arguments, the reality is that online privacy is quite a conundrum, a paradox even.

According to the Federal Trade Commission (FTC), millions of netizens fall victim to different kinds of criminal activities online each year. It could be anything from identity theft to outright fraud. Yet, the funny thing is that the internet is awash with alarming statistics and information on cybercrime, tips on how to stay safe online, and how to detect potential fraud from afar. How is it, therefore, that in this information age, people still fall victim to cybercriminals?

Therein lies the paradox, because while there's been widespread concern and alarm about privacy online, and despite the access to resources we can use for fact-checking, a lot of users still willingly, and intentionally engage in risky behavior online, exposing their privileged information to criminals in the process. It's quite funny, that the very people claiming concern about privacy online make it so easy for criminals to access not just their data, but their entire digital lives. We know what to do to stay safe but still act in a manner that negates the very concept of online privacy that we desire. This explains why more than 40 million consumers in the US fell victim to identity theft in 2021.

To understand the severity of these concerns, let's first explore the dynamics of digital identity, and why you should pay attention.

Your Digital Identity

We all have unique physical identities that, for example, can help you tell identical twins apart. For example, their unique behavior, voice, and other physical attributes like their walking style. Without knowledge of such, it would be difficult to tell one from the other. Physical identity, therefore, is mostly about physical attributes.

Digital identities, on the other hand, are reusable, digital proof of your behavior, digital characteristics, personal information, and other details of your physical identity, for example, your blood group, eye color, height, and so on. While both digital and physical identities provide useful information about you, digital identities give more insight at a glance than physical identities ever will.

For example, from your medical insurance card, someone could easily figure out your current health status, based on the information they can access. Digital identities are part and parcel of our existence in the technological age and play an important role in enabling and supporting access to various online services like healthcare, government services, online retail, and financial inclusion. Just like their physical counterparts, digital identities are unique to each individual and prove that you are who you say you are.

Digital identities are further split into two categories, attributes and activities. Attributes are features that are unique to each individual. For example, your medical history, date of birth, driver's license, Social Security number, bank account details, and biometric information like your iris scan or fingerprint.

Digital activities, on the other hand, represent your footprint in the digital world, but you might not necessarily be responsible for them. For example, your online purchase history, posts, comments, and likes on social media, petitions you've signed, campaigns you support, and your search history. While these activities could be associated with your accounts, someone else could be responsible for them.

Importance of Digital Identity Security

Given that your digital activities might not necessarily be your true activities, you have to take your digital security seriously. A lot of people have ended up on the wrong side of the law for digital activities that they were not aware of, usually as a result of identity theft.

Let's say one of your friends uses your phone to threaten someone online, and the victim decides to press charges. The threats will be tracked down to you through your phone's IP address, and the social media account registered in your name. Unfortunately, you were not responsible for the trouble that was coming your way. This is how a lot of people have ended up paying fines or worse, serving jail time for crimes they never committed, or had no clue about.

The value and relevance of digital identity become more apparent as the world continues to hinge on technology. Digital identities provide so much more information about you at a glance than physical identities do, which explains the drive for the widespread digitization of identities worldwide. Many countries have or are actively adopting digital identities at the moment.

Other than overcoming the cumbersome nature of physical identities, digital identities are easier to manage, more afford-able, and give authorities an easier time tracking down criminals. However, digital identities are not risk-free. There's always the risk of data breaches with far-reaching effects. For example, imagine what would happen if your insurer was hacked. The criminals would have access to privileged information on millions of people, including their addresses, medical history, financial records, employment data, and so on. Such information is quite valuable, depending on what the criminals intend to do with it.

One of the biggest digital identity risks is identity theft. It's quite a nightmare because, in capable hands, criminals could create a whole new person using your digital identity. Once that process is complete, you can never tell what your digital clone will be up to. You plan for a vacation with your family, only to be surprised at the airport when the FBI swoops in to arrest you, citing a ridiculous list of crimes that you apparently have been committing. You can imagine the trauma on your family, and more importantly, the chaos and disruption this will have on your life by the time you clear your name if you ever manage to do so.

The Future is Digital

The potential risks notwithstanding, digital identity is here, and it is the future. Evidence of this is in the way various countries are fast-tracking efforts towards creating digital identity databases. Digital identity is like AI, it is here, and it continues to evolve, capturing more details about your life, online or otherwise.

It's not a seamless ecosystem yet, but humanity in general is taking significant strides towards building safe, reliable, accurate, and resilient digital identities. For example, there are lots of technicalities and legal landmines that we must navigate to fully implement digital identities. This lays the infrastructure and framework for interactive engagement between individuals, businesses, governments, and any other entity.

Finally, there's the issue of identity ownership. In the formative stages, digital identities are mostly owned by the entities building the ecosystems where the identities reside. However, these identities can only become effective when ownership is passed down to the individual owners. This is where the privacy paradox comes in. We must create awareness around digital identities so that we take proactive steps in safeguarding our identities online. This is how digital identities become a reality.

The Paradox: Privacy in a Public Online Domain

From identity theft to corporate data breaches, online privacy is an issue we tackle every other day, at a personal, professional, and corporate level. If you know what to look for, you can learn so much about anyone online in a few minutes. Therein comes the paradox. How does a generation that lives most of its lives online stay private without disrupting the balance? On top of that, what is online privacy, and is it a myth, or something achievable?

There are many ways to describe online privacy. The consensus in every description, however, revolves around the amount of your browsing, financial, and personal data you keep private while you are online. This data must be kept private because, in the wrong hands, someone can easily create a new digital identity that takes a life of its own once it's out there.

Take a moment and think about the things you share online about your life. Sure, at times it feels good to post your wins on social media, but imagine what criminals can do with that information. By criminals, we're not just talking about hackers. Anyone could find value in the information you share online.

Kidnappers, for example, now know where your kids go to school, where you live, where you work, your car registration plate, your family members and where they live, and so on. It's quite scary, and that's why we must all take a step back and rethink the kind of information we share online.

Can we truly achieve the utmost privacy in the public domain?

This is an interesting question, a contentious one at best, and one that has been divisive for centuries, long before the internet came about. People have been concerned about privacy since as early as the 1890s. The concept of privacy is quite simple, the integrity, confidentiality, and ease of access to certain information. These three aspects are influenced by how information is collected, processed, stored, and disseminated. At the heart of it all, lies security. Your data will never be private without appropriate security measures.

In the digital age, it's fair to say that nothing can truly ever be private. After all, even if you use the strongest security measures, you're still sharing your information with someone, whether it's encrypted or not.

Big players in the tech industry have found themselves on the wrong side of the law, both legal and public opinion on the issue of privacy. From the National Security Agency (NSA) to Meta Platforms (formerly Facebook), data and access are thorny issues that never seem to go away. It gets worse when you think of the current gold rush, where every company is trying to gather some information about users, for different reasons. Someone's always listening, from the conversations you have at home, to your chats on your phone, there's always something valuable someone could derive from that data, and the biggest culprit is the advertising industry.

You're thinking of upgrading your home entertainment experience with the latest smart TV, but what you don't know is that the very source of excitement you're excited about could be used to spy on you. Say you buy a smart TV from company A, who also happens to manufacture the phone you are using. They could listen in on your conversations, and suddenly, you start noticing suggestive ads on your phone. Ads are no longer random. To be effective, advertisers must try to be as accurate as possible, increasing the chances that you'll make a purchase. It's all about the money, well mostly.

Here's another interesting fact. CIA hackers executed zero-day hacks to exploit vulnerabilities in some of the popular messaging apps that encrypt your communication. They also penetrated some antivirus systems. Of course, the concerned entities might have found workarounds by now, but the fact that the CIA could do it means that there are hackers out there who could equally do the same, and not for the kind of reasons the CIA did.

How is Your Data Collected?

Given the privacy paradox, and the reality that your data might not be as private as different entities would wish you to believe, it might be useful to learn about the kind of data you hemorrhage online, and how it is collected. While you might not be able to get 100% privacy online, you can still take measures to limit your exposure and protect your digital identity.

Businesses, for example, collect the following data:

- Attitude data - This includes your sentiments, purchase patterns, and satisfaction with certain products or services.
- Behavioral data - Your activity online, such as browsing history, how you use certain digital products or services, subscriptions, and so on. This also includes monitoring your clicks and engagement on different websites.
- Engagement data - The objective here is to understand how you interact with their online presence, from their emails, ads, social media pages, mobile apps, and so on.
- Personal data - Anything that can be used to verify your identity, including your IP address, gender, name, address, Social Security Number, and so on.

Businesses are interested in this data because it helps them refine their processes efficiently. At the end of the day, their goal is to make as much money as possible, so it's in their best interest to understand you and everything else that happens in your purchase journey.

But, how do they obtain this information?

Well, companies can be direct about it, and ask you to provide feedback, or share some information when signing up for their business. Alternatively, they could also employ indirect methods, which essentially mean tracking your every move online.

Unfortunately, other than using your information to refine their business practices, companies also sell your personal information. This is currently one of the most lucrative ventures, the ethical challenges notwithstanding. Sadly, once your data is sold, it can be resold perpetually to many other entities.

Privacy Policies

Like Terms and Conditions, most people never read Privacy Policies. We simply agree and proceed, oblivious of the content of the policy statement. A privacy policy document provides a legal explanation of how the company intends to collect, use, and process your data on its website or app. Many companies try to simplify the policies as much as possible so that it's easier for you to comprehend. However, a good number still have the complex legal jargon that would bore you to death. That notwithstanding, it is an important statement that you should spare time and read.

Businesses generally collect information relevant to their core objective. Some of the information they collect includes:

- Your full names
- Billing and mailing addresses
- Contact information
- Age
- Sex
- Nationality
- Payment information

You should always read privacy policies because the US, for example, does not have a national privacy law that applies to such cases. However, some states do, so if you're running an online business, it would be wise to understand how the law in your jurisdiction applies to the kind of business you own. The same applies to customers, so you understand the legal protections you enjoy within your state when engaging business online. Beyond the US, global businesses also come under the microscope. For example, businesses operating in Europe must comply with the General Data Protection Regulation (GDPR).

For businesses, the consequences of flouting regulation can be dire. Take the case of X (formerly Twitter), which was fined $150 million in 2022 for using the phone numbers people register for two-factor authentication, for advertising.

That's as serious as things can get. Even though the relevant authorities, for example, the FTC, might not have the resources to take on every business that mishandles user data, you could still be sued in any court that can litigate privacy concerns, and you might pay a hefty fine for that.

Social media, for example, is one place where many businesses mishandle user data without necessarily realizing their mistake. We share so much of our lives online, and at times, businesses do the same without consent from the parties involved. There have been many instances where such businesses are brought to book, in the process, raising awareness on the importance of privacy and consent.

At the end of the day, privacy comes down to security. Unless you give express consent, someone can only access and use your digital material if they obtained it illegally. Here are some simple tips that can help you keep your data safe on social media:

- Check your privacy settings from time to time, to make sure you're sharing data with the right people, whether it's friends, family, or people who fit your desired demographics.
- As easy as it might seem, never enable auto login on social media. This grants anyone who has your device instant access to your accounts.
- Turn on two-factor authentication.
- Update your security questions regularly, and make sure the answers are not easy to guess.
- Use a VPN service to obscure your data when you're online.
- Make sure your antivirus is updated.
- Use a strong password, and change it regularly.
- Don't just accept all friend requests. Some requests come from pseudo accounts, whose intentions might not be genuine.
- Do not tag your location on your photos and videos.
- Never share personal information on social media.
- Avoid clicking links, even if they are shared by people you know. Criminals like to use social media to push their phishing links because of how easily we trust people in our circles.

- If you suspect an account is fake, trust your gut and block it right away.
- Always investigate suspicious login attempts and change your login details right away.
- Do not allow your browser to save your login details. If someone hacks your device, they can easily sign into your accounts.
- If you haven't used an account in years, and probably won't use it, close it. Idle accounts are easy targets for hackers, and in most cases, they are not usually well-protected.

As you can see from our discussion above, utmost privacy is not something anyone can guarantee you online. There's only so much that the companies and digital products we engage online can do to guarantee safety. Beyond that, the biggest burden rests on your shoulders. You must take the initiative to protect your digital identity and use all the tools available. More importantly, be mindful and conscious about what you share online.

The internet is permanent. Once you post something online, it lives on forever, whether you delete it or not. People take and keep screenshots, and save your photos and videos for different reasons. So, always remember that as soon as you post something online, it takes a life of its own, and will outlive you.

Why You Should Never Overshare

One thing that comes out clearly in the paradox of privacy is that in most cases, we become the architects of our undoing. For example, even though we're fully aware of the risks of illegal downloads, we still flock to Torrent networks for illegal copies of movies, our favorite TV shows, games, and other software.

The same problem is common on social media. One of the greatest dangers of social media is that we tend to share more than we should. Social media is awesome and has been a great asset to millions of people. It allows us to connect with friends, families, colleagues, business associates, customers, and strangers on various levels. Social media is such an important part of our lives that some financial service providers even consider your social media activity when assessing your credit position.

Despite all that, social media has its ills, some unique to their design, and others the result of human nature. The fact that you can be anything and anyone you want on social media creates room for a lot of fallacies. You can build a new persona online and give it a life of its own. People fake lives on social media for attention. Unfortunately, not all attention is good for you.

While we have so much fun on social media, most people never stop to understand the psychological aspect of it. Attention is the most valuable currency on social media. That's why advertisers pay a lot of money to feature on your timelines. It's all about organic engagements, and that's where we at times lose the plot and share more information than we should.

Oversharing on social media is a pandemic on its own. It's normal to get caught up in the excitement when something good is happening in your life, but at the same time, you must be careful not to give off more information than necessary. Whether it's good or bad news, the emotions get in the way, blinding you to the reality that you might be giving off privileged information to strangers.

How much is too much?

Well, this is subjective, because circumstances differ from one person to the next. However, you need to be mindful of the kind of information you put online, and how it might be used against you in the future. Know that anyone could save your photos and videos, or even keep screenshots for future reference. More importantly, just because people are happy and excited for you online doesn't necessarily mean that they are truly happy in real life. You never know who feels threatened by your success.

For example, many people use social media to express their emotional frustrations. You could even share how depressed you feel about something you're going through. While you can get a lot of emotional support and encouragement online, someone could also use this moment of weakness to scam their way into your life, pretending to be going through something similar.

The easiest way to avoid putting yourself in such situations is to be mindful of what you share online. At the end of the day, you are in charge of your online accounts, so you must be keen on what you put out there. Before you share anything personal online, think twice about the ramifications of that post. For example, ask yourself whether that information reveals something personal about you or someone close to you. Will your post offend someone? At times the damage isn't immediate, but could become apparent in a few months or years. After all, the internet never forgets.

Engage your friends and family members and ask them to delete any comments or photos that could be offensive or link back to you in a bad way. You might not have put the post up yourself, but in the age of social media, a lot of people have suffered the consequences of guilt by association. Social media users hardly ever wait to hear both sides of the story. The most sensational version always carries the day.

Review your contact list on social media and delete users that you do not like. This might seem a bit melodramatic, but think about it for a moment. Why would you give someone you don't like front-row seats to your personal life? Prune your social media circles depending on the nature of your relationships.

Understand and explain boundaries to your friends and family members. People take photos and videos at parties and post them online without giving it much thought. However, most don't realize that once the content is published, it takes a life of its own, and spreads so fast all over the world. What seemed like an innocent prank could be the very thing that destroys your professional career or even some personal relationships. Respect each other's privacy, just as much as you'd wish to have yours respected.

Passwords and Authentication

Your password is the gateway to your online identity. You must implement smart safeguards around your passwords so they don't fall into the wrong hands. Password protection is the first, and most important step in keeping all your accounts safe and secure. Criminals invest in high-end tech to try and hack online accounts, hence the need for you to take password security seriously. Imagine the risk you'd be exposed to if someone had access to any of your accounts today.

The point of password security is to make things as difficult as possible for potential criminals. This, in some cases, could also mean making things difficult for you too. For example, many people use passwords that they can easily remember, like their year of birth, names of their kids or pets, favorite foods, and so on. While these are easy to commit to memory, they are also easy for hackers to penetrate. Here are some simple tips to help you protect your passwords, and by extension, your digital identity:

- Keep your password as private as your ATM PIN. Don't even share it with your friends or family members.
- Never use the same password for multiple accounts. This is quite risky and could leave you exposed on multiple fronts.
- Make your passwords as long as possible, using at least 16 characters. This makes it harder to guess or hack.
- The harder it is to guess your password, the better. But, at the same time, try to use passwords that you can easily remember, or use a password manager if you choose passwords longer than 16 characters.
- If possible, make use of multi-factor authentication (MFA), also known as two-factor authentication (2FA). This is an additional layer of protection in case someone cracks your password.
- Do not use the word password or any iteration of it as your password, for example, Password32. Similarly, do not use your name in your password, or the name of anyone you know or engage frequently, like your kids, parents, or partner.

- An ideal password should be a combination of uppercase letters, lowercase letters, numbers, and symbols.

We mentioned the use of password managers earlier. Password management tools can come in handy if you're not sure how to create a strong password. For most of them, all you have to do is select the number of characters, and character combinations, then they generate a strong password for you. Note, however, that given the treasure trove of information held within password management tools, they're constantly targeted by hackers hoping to extract some valuable information. That being said, no one is fully immune from hacking attempts, so you're better off trying some of the functionalities of password management tools than not using them at all. Here are some good examples you can look into:

- LastPass: https://lastpass.com/
- KeePass: https://keepass.info/
- Keeper: https://keepersecurity.com/
- Password Safe: https://pwsafe.org/
- Dashlane: https://dashlane.com/

If you choose to use password managers or any other password management solution, always make sure you use different passwords for each of the password management accounts.

Multi-factor Authentication (MFA)

You have probably come across one or more of these tools, and might even have one on your phone right now. Good examples include the Dashlane Authenticator app and the Google Authenticator app. MFA is a security approach to ensure that you need more than one authentication point to access your account. This means that your password alone cannot guarantee a hacker access.

From our discussion on password security, you've probably highlighted a few mistakes you've made with your passwords. For example, you might have one password across several accounts, you could also have admin123 or some other iteration as your password, and so on. Such passwords are easy to break, giving anyone easy access to your accounts.

With MFA, someone would have to hack your phone to receive your messages or get your phone to retrieve the authentication code, on top of your password. In short, having your password is not enough. They must also find you physically to retrieve the second layer protocols; since that's not possible, your account is safe.

MFA generally comes into effect if you try to access your account from a new device, IP address, or location, or if you're signing in soon after resetting your password. This is to prove that you're the one trying to access the account. Beyond that, you'll only need your password. You could, however, change the individual app or account settings to require MFA each time you sign in. It might seem quite an inconvenience, but in the long run, it's for your good. Some platforms, like PayPal, require an MFA each time you sign in.

The Dashlane Authenticator app, for example, uses time-based one-time passwords (TOTP), set to 30 seconds. This means that the code generated by the authenticator app is only valid for 30 seconds, after which the app generates another.

Guide to Using Dashlane Authenticator

Download and install the Dashlane Authenticator from your app store. Click on Get Started, and create a Master Password. That's the password that grants you access to your authenticator. Dashlane will not store your Master Password, so choose a strong one, but make sure it's something you can remember.

Your screen should look like this:

Next, enter your Master Password again to confirm and create your account. If you don't wish to use the Master Password, you could also create a passwordless account. However, given everything we've discussed about passwords and protecting your digital identity, it's safer to create a Master Password.

The next step is optional. Instead of using your Master Password to access your Dashlane Authenticator, you can enable biometric access. This will use whichever biometric systems your phone supports, whether it's an iris scan, or a fingerprint lock, as shown below.

Once you've set your biometrics as desired, press continue and enter the email address you'd wish to associate with your authenticator. Read and agree to the terms of service and privacy policy then proceed as shown below:

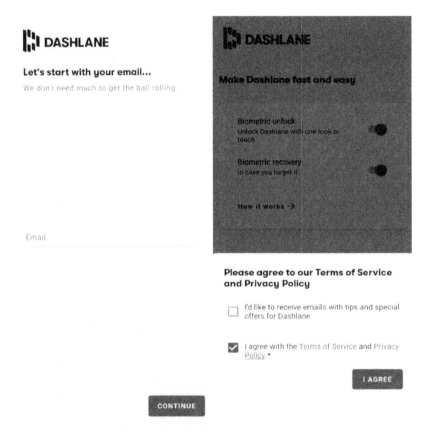

After agreeing to the privacy policy, the authenticator will ease you into the settings depending on your experience with password managers. This makes the setup process seamless whether it is your first time or you've had some experience with password managers before.

Choose from the appropriate settings shown, and customize your settings as you wish.

Add the logins, activate autofill if you don't wish to enter your details all the time, then connect your computer, and you'll be good to go.

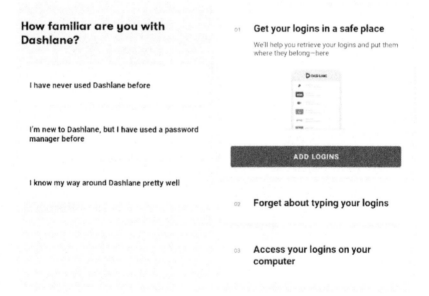

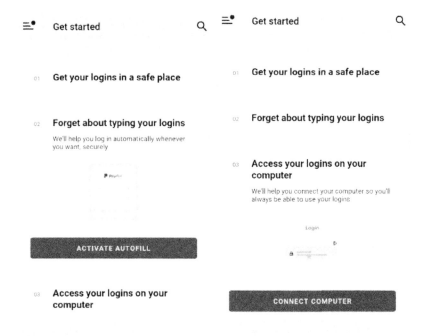

Your account is ready, so you can fiddle with it and learn more. At this point, you have a free account, which still works, but you can upgrade to the premium version and access more features.

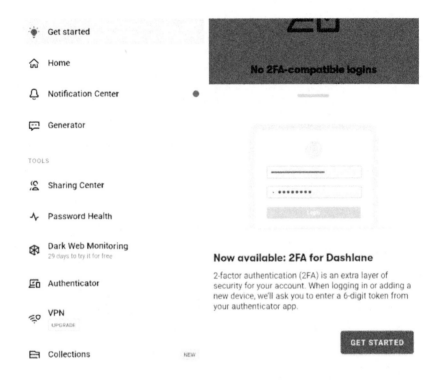

Click on Get Started to enable two-factor authentication.

Once you Add New Login, Dashlane will populate a list of accounts that you can secure. You can either scroll down the list to find the service you need or use the search box to find what you need.

In this case, we're looking for Gmail.

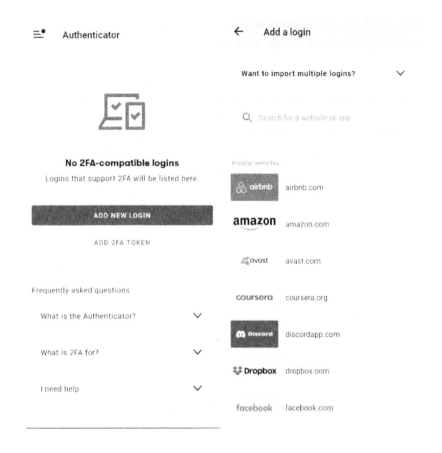

Sign into your Gmail account and the authenticator will save your details.

You can also enable autofill to ease the sign-in process for your accounts as shown below.

Your Gmail account is now completely set, and ready to go.

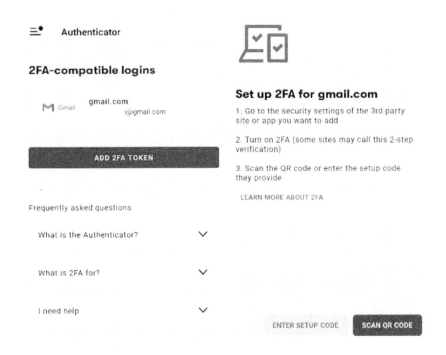

Guide to Using Google Authenticator

Google Authenticator is one of the most frequently used authenticators in the market and is fairly straightforward to use. Most apps, websites, and programs use Google Authenticator as their default service for two-factor authentication.

Download the app and sign in with your Google account.

Scan a QR code or enter the setup key to load the account you wish to protect as shown below.

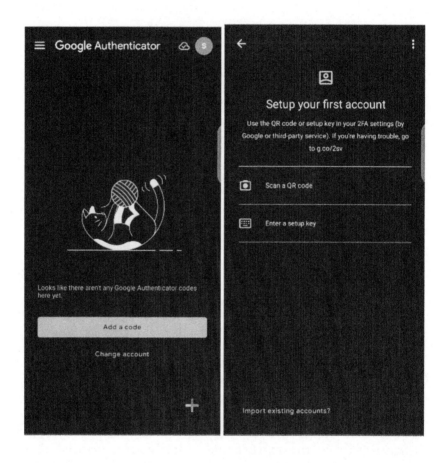

Select Import Existing Accounts if you have the authenticator created for other accounts, and would wish to have them all in one place.

If you already have the authenticator installed on an older phone, you can transfer the settings to your new phone from the menu as shown below, then follow the simple instructions to complete the transfer.

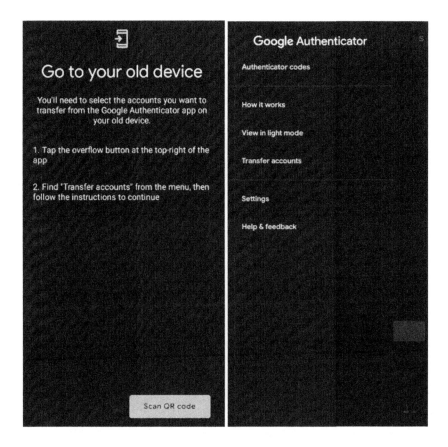

Even though each website or app that supports MFA has different settings, you can set it up in one or two steps from the app/website settings page, select two-factor authentication, and follow the prompts on your screen.

If you wish to learn more about privacy online and how to protect your digital identity and assets online, the Federal Trade Commission (FTC) has some useful material that can add a lot of value to your life.

Interactive Element

Q1. Why is multi-factor authentication important?

Multi-factor authentication adds an extra layer of security beyond just using passwords. Even if your password is compromised, having an additional authentication factor significantly reduces the risk of unauthorized access. It enhances overall account security and helps protect against various cyber threats like phishing and credential theft.

Q2. Why must you protect your digital identity?

Protecting digital identity is crucial to prevent identity theft, fraud, and unauthorized access to personal information or accounts. A secure digital identity framework ensures privacy, security, and trust in online transactions and interactions, reducing the risk of identity-related cyber threats.

Q3. What makes up your digital identity?

Digital identity can consist of various components, including personal information (name, date of birth, etc.), online account credentials (usernames, passwords), biometric data (fingerprints, facial recognition), digital certificates, and unique identifiers like Social Security Numbers or government-issued IDs.

Well, there you have it. Your privacy online, in a nutshell, comes down to the choice you make. Your digital identity is just as important as your passport and Social Security Number, so you have to protect it by all means necessary. There are tools, and resources you can use, but at the end of the day, it all comes down to the decisions you make, the websites you visit, the apps you download, and so on. Now that you understand how important your privacy is, let's dive in, and talk about how to stay safe online, in the next chapter.

5

Clicks, Links, and Tricks: The Guide to Safe Browsing

The internet is an interesting place. Think of it like your first time in an electrifying, bustling city. It's a mix of excitement and uncertainty. There are so many unknowns, yet at the same time, it's filled with opportunities for endless exploration. When you come to the city, you have to worry about all kinds of criminals who could take advantage of you, especially if you don't know your way around. However, even those who've lived in the city longer than you've been there still fall victim to criminals from time to time. You must be cautious, trust no one, and make sure you know where you're going, or at least, ask someone you can trust. But, who can you trust?

The same concept applies to the internet. Whether you're a beginner, or you're tech savvy, there's always a criminal lurking in the shadows, hoping that you become their next prey. The only way you can be safe is to take proactive measures to protect yourself while you're online. The truth is that you can't be 100% safe online. However, given this realization, there are steps you can take to make sure you're not a sitting duck. In the unlikely event that a criminal attempts to exploit you, you'll spot them from a mile away and avoid them like a plague.

In this chapter, we explore the security dynamics of the second digital dimension—digital consumption. The internet is an important part of our lives today, so in most cases, we cannot do without it. It's important, therefore, that you learn useful strategies to protect yourself and your online activities from risky browsing behavior.

Think of the internet like your body. If you engage in risky, careless, and promiscuous behavior, there's a good chance you'll catch something that will destroy your life. On the other hand, if you protect yourself and are cautious with the people you interact with, you could live a long and healthy life. The secret is to never take your security and safety for granted.

What's Safe and What's Dangerous When Browsing Online?

You're exposed to risks each time you come online. Whether you're on your phone, computer, video game, or any other device that can access the internet, danger lurks all around you. With that in mind, here are some useful safety tips to enhance your online experience:

- Always be mindful of what you post on social media. You never know who's watching, or their intentions.
- Keep all software and apps updated so you're always protected with the latest security fixes and updates.
- Never open suspicious attachments or documents, and if you have to, open them on Google Drive or Chrome because they can scan for malware.
- Ensure all URLs are secure before you click on the link. A secure URL starts with https:// and should have a lock icon on the address bar.
- To verify authenticity, long-press the link text on your phone or hover your cursor over the link.
- Activate two-step authentication on any platform where it's available, and use strong passwords for all your accounts.

- If you receive an email or message that seems too good to be true, it probably is. Make a habit of searching the name of the sender online to verify their identity. You can also add words like hoax, scam, or con alongside the name to bring up any relevant searches of the same.

Now that you know what to do, here are some useful tips on what not to do online:

- Never open or respond to suspicious emails.
- Never click on suspicious links or anything you don't trust, including videos, photos, and memes.
- Never use one password across all or multiple accounts. If someone gains access to one account, they could easily infiltrate all your related accounts.
- Avoid public Wi-Fi hotspots and public computers. If you have to use them, do not pay for anything online through such networks.
- Be careful where you sign in, and if you're using public services, like computers and Wi-Fi hotspots, do not share your personal information.
- Never allow unrestricted access to personal data from apps you do not trust.
- Some people might think you're hiding something, but make a good habit of not leaving your phone screen or computer unlocked. Set up automatic screen locks just in case you step away briefly and forget to lock them.

Safe Browsing Best Practices

The do's and don'ts we discussed above can only get you so far. As online criminals keep getting smarter and more daring by the day, you must also have a few tricks up your sleeve. Here are some simple tips that can help you identify dangerous links and websites:

- Run a quick search for that website on WHOIS. This will show you to whom the website is registered and could protect you from scammers who clone websites and lure unsuspecting users.
- For online transactions, never pay money into someone's bank account. There's a good chance you'll never see your money. To be safe, use credit cards, or secure third-party platforms like PayPal, which offer security if things don't work out.
- If a website is promising or offering you something that seems too good to be true, it is. If the promise is as easy as they say it is, why don't they do it themselves?
- Always research new websites to find out what other users think about them. Read reviews, but be careful because many websites buy or pay for good reviews to hoodwink unsuspecting users. Besides, if the website is relatively new, it might not have any reviews yet.
- Make sure you are accessing the website from a secure connection. As we mentioned earlier, secure websites should have the padlock symbol and https on the address. Even so, you must still take a few steps to ensure you're not interacting through a cloned website.

- Criminals usually buy domain names that look similar to popular websites, so follow all the steps we've listed to verify their authenticity, especially if you need to conduct financial transactions online.

While these measures will easily protect you, this doesn't mean that you should let your guard down once you've followed them. The digital space evolves rapidly, and criminals come up with new tactics every day. Be vigilant, and never take anything for granted.

Download, Upload, and Share Files Securely

Other than casual browsing, most online activity involves downloading, uploading, or sharing files. This, unfortunately, is also where criminals lay traps. What might seem like a harmless meme could be hiding malware that will destroy your devices. Remember the story of the Trojan horse? The wooden horse the Greeks used during the Trojan War to gain entry into the City of Troy, and eventually won the war. Well, that's how criminals conceal their intentions. There's a reason why some of the worst malware are trojans because, at first glance, they seem harmless. You download or even install them on your devices, when in the real sense, what you see is a smokescreen. Behind the scenes, irreparable damage could be taking place.

Here are some simple guidelines to help you stay vigilant in case you're downloading, uploading, or sharing any files online:

- Always run a virus scan on files before you download them, even if they were sent to you by someone you trust, or downloaded from a website you trust.
- Keep your antivirus and firewall software up to date.
- Use legitimate websites to download things like music, games, or video content.
- Your friends or associates might not be the best people to advise you on the security of a website. Trust your gut instinct, and if anything looks sketchy, don't use it.
- Close all important programs and apps before you download anything. This way, you reduce the risk of crashing and losing data if the download isn't successful.
- If you need to install multiple apps or programs, do it one by one. It's easier to identify a problematic program this way than if you had multiple installations running concurrently.
- While most people don't do this, try to read the instructions before downloading or installing applications online. Terms and conditions might be lengthy, but there's a reason why they were created, and you can only proceed once you agree to the terms.
- Do not accept anything that promises you freebies, or to transform your computer into something it isn't, for example, an Xbox.

The tips above are simple guidelines. To stay safe online, you must be proactive in everything you do. Remember that nothing is free, and if anyone is offering you something for free, then you most certainly are the product.

Here's a list of trusted software and websites that you can use to share, download, upload or manage files online:

- Cloud storage platforms like Dropbox, Google Drive, and Microsoft OneDrive.
- Chat apps like WhatsApp and Telegram Messenger.
- Use programs like WinZip and 7-Zip to compress large files into smaller sizes that you can easily send online.
- Use VPN services to conceal the destination and size of the file you're trying to send, in case your internet service provider (ISP) has limitations.
- Transfer the file physically on a USB flash drive. Be careful though, because this is also one of the easiest ways to transfer a virus from infected computers.
- Use Jumpshare, WeTransfer, or Send Anywhere to create shareable links for any files you'd wish to transfer.

At the end of the day, you must be careful when sharing files online, or accessing shared files. Take precautions and scan all files before you download or open them. More importantly, keep your antivirus scanners updated at all times.

Safe Browsing for Children and the Elderly

Just as we try to understand the psychology of criminals, they also do the same for the rest of us. Criminals understand that tech-savvy internet users constantly try to learn how to outsmart them, so smart criminals stay away from you as soon as they get the slightest hint that you might have figured them out.

So, what do they do next? They look for easy prey, internet users who might be naive and unsuspecting. They go after kids and the elderly. In this demographic, you get users who are too trusting and can easily fall for the simplest online scams. For this reason, you have a duty of care to the kids and elderly in your household. Given your knowledge of cybercrime, you should take proactive measures to protect your loved ones. Let's explore some simple guidelines you can implement to keep your household safe:

Protecting Your Kids

Create awareness about responsible online behavior in your household. There are lots of teachable moments in this, suitable for both kids and the elderly. Talk to them about boundaries, and simple rules on what they should or should not do online.

Of course, there's so much to learn about online security than you can cover in one teachable moment, so try not to rush this. Remember that online security is a vastly evolving concern, so you should not approach this as a one-time thing. Each time you come across some useful information, share it with them and show them how to identify legitimate online activities from criminal activities. More importantly, encourage them to reach out whenever they come across something they feel is suspicious, or if they are ever unsure of something.

The most important thing is to raise awareness, especially for your children. This is about more than preparing them for what they interact with right now, but mostly about preparing them for what they might experience in the future. As your kids grow up, you won't always be there to protect them from what they access online. Kids grow up and become more adventurous, taking more risks online than you could ever imagine. If you impart the right online culture in them right now, it's easier for them to make better choices as they grow up, because they know not only what's right and wrong, but also why they need to be responsible and accountable for their actions online, and the repercussions of not doing so.

Here's a link to SOS, an intuitive online game by the FBI that teaches kids basic skills to keep them safe online. The game is simple and informative, and you can also enjoy it, not just your kids.

Next, teach your kids about search engines. While Google might be your go-to search engine, it's not necessarily the safest place for your kids. Google Scholar, however, is a safe ad-free search engine for academic articles. This, unfortunately, might be useful for kids in advanced classes. Not to worry though, as there are some great solutions for younger kids too. Here's a list of some kid-friendly search engines you can explore with your children:

- Fact Monster
- SweetSearch
- Kidtopia
- KidRex
- KidzSearch
- Kiddle

Finally, you need to learn the importance of setting up parental controls in your household. Parental controls are device or software-level options that give you control over your children's internet activity. You can monitor what your kids do online, and even block inappropriate material that could have bypassed the safety measures put in place by the developers.

Parental controls can be implemented at different levels, and are available for everything from your operating system, browser, video streaming apps, search engines, smartphones, and gaming devices. Even though parental controls give you peace of mind knowing what your kids are up to, you must still be vigilant, since nothing is ever 100% safe online. Besides, criminals also understand how parental controls work, and are always looking for ways of circumventing the security measures to entrap your kids.

Before introducing your kids to any internet-enabled device or solution, find out about their parental control protocols, and how to set them up. The settings vary for every manufacturer or developer, so take your time and learn how each of them works before allowing your kids to use them. At the end of the day, you will always be your child's first and best line of defense.

Protecting The Elderly

The kids are safe, so let's now look at how to protect the elderly in your household. While they're both vulnerable to criminals, the elderly have something that kids might not have—money! Older adults could even be more vulnerable to criminals online than kids because they might not be open to talking about their online activities.

For example, if they have a gambling problem, it's highly unlikely that they'll open up to you and tell you they were conned online while trying to win big at some online casino. They'll keep this to themselves, and probably look for more money to try and win back what they lost, not realizing that they are being scammed. Here are some common scams targeting the elderly that you should be aware of:

- **Romance Scams**

You might be wondering why an elderly person whose best years are long gone could fall for a romance scam. Well, the answer is quite simple—loneliness. Criminals target your weakest spots, and loneliness is one of those things that make us all vulnerable at some point. Think about it, wouldn't it be amazing to have someone in your sunset years, someone who understands you, cares for you, and reminds you that you've lived a good life?

Well, that's how criminals reel in the elderly. They create accounts on social media and dating sites, then profile unsuspecting victims. After engaging the victim for a while, the criminal will pretend to be overseas, and excited to meet their newfound love. The victim is usually asked to send money for random things, like a medical emergency, a visa, or anything else that the criminal can come up with.

- **Lottery and Charity Scams**

In this case, the criminals will call to inform the victim that they won some lottery, but there's a catch. To receive their winnings, the victim would have to send them some money, or gift cards to offset processing fees, taxes, and other things that might come up. To gain the victim's trust, many of these criminals usually portray themselves as employees of popular companies.

- **Tech Support Scams**

The concept here is quite simple. The criminals assume that older people don't know so much about cybersecurity or computers in general. If you happen to access one of their pages or download something on your laptop or phone that installs a virus on your system, your screen goes blank, or you get a notification that something's wrong with your device. This is usually accompanied by a "tech support" number. When you call the number, the criminal will either ask you to pay some money so they can fix the problem on your device, or share instructions that will give them remote access to your device.

If you ever have any issue, legitimate tech support will never ask you for money over the phone to fix your problem. In most cases ask you to bring the device to their offices. Upon diagnosis by their experts, they will then advise you on how to proceed, and costs if applicable. Anyone who tries to remotely access your device might be well aware of your online accounts and are simply trying to access them.

- **Grandchild Scam**

The grandchild scam targets the close bonds that grandparents have with their grandkids. In this case, the criminal will call the grandparent, asking them to guess who it is. When the grandparent says a name, they pick up on it and set the trap. The criminal then claims to be in some trouble and needs the grandparent to bail them out, but requests that it remains a secret so the parents will never find out.

It's usually quite an elaborate scam, and in some cases, the criminals might even have someone come to the grandparent's door, pretending to be a courier to collect the money. In some cases, the criminals pretend to be professionals like doctors, police officers, or lawyers, trying to assist the "grandchild" in distress.

- **Government Imposter Scam**

This scam usually involves some threats to urge the victim into action. For example, the criminals will pretend to be from Medicare, the Social Security Administration, the Internal

Revenue Service (IRS), or any other government agency. They then threaten the victim with deportation, arrest, or being cut off from receiving the relevant government services if they do not clear their bills, or share some personal information with the criminals.

The coercion usually works for the unsuspecting victim. The criminals will either receive the money and run, or use the personal information shared with them for identity theft and other crimes. In 2022, criminals made away with more than $720 million through tech support and government imposter scams, and that's only from scamming people older than 60 years. Interestingly enough, while there were victims in younger age groups, the amount lost by the elderly was still far greater than the total loss from all the other age groups, which highlights the fact that criminals continue to exploit this group because of its vulnerability.

Recommended Antivirus Software

One of the most important things as far as internet security is concerned, is to have legitimate and updated antivirus software running on your devices. By legitimate, I mean buying the software from the official provider. Do not use illegal patches or cracks obtained from torrent networks or other file-sharing platforms. Here's a list of some of the most trusted and highly recommended antivirus programs:

Avast

Trusted by more than 400 million users all over the world, Avast has been around since 1995 and provides various security solutions for PC, Mac, and Android devices against online threats, including viruses, malware, spyware, ransomware, and phishing attacks.

Pros

- Avast offers real-time protection against malware, viruses, spyware, and ransomware, detecting threats as they occur.
- You get multiple scanning options, including full system scans, targeted scans, and customizable scans, so you can always choose the depth and focus of the scan.
- Their Wi-Fi Inspector identifies vulnerabilities in your network and connected devices, ensuring a more secure internet connection, for example, it will alert you if you have a weak Wi-Fi password.
- Avast monitors the behavior of applications and programs in real-time, identifying and stopping suspicious activities.
- You can use the password manager to securely store and manage passwords for your accounts.
- You have a dedicated mode that minimizes interruptions and notifications when you are playing games or using full-screen applications.

- It's one of the antivirus programs with a commendable user interface, making it an easy solution for both beginners and expert users.

Cons

- Avast has been known to consume a significant amount of system resources, leading to slowdowns, especially if you have an old device or one with low specs.
- The free versions of Avast occasionally display pop-up ads prompting you to upgrade to the premium version. Ads are always quite intrusive.
- Avast has faced criticism for data collection practices that some users consider invasive, although the company has made efforts to be more transparent about data usage.
- Some of the more advanced features, for example, firewall and other extra privacy tools, are available only in the paid versions, so even though the free version is quite sufficient for most users, you might have to pay up to enjoy advanced features.

Price starts at $49.99 for the first year, though the free version also offers ample protection. Download it from their official website https://www.avast.com/

Avira

Avira has been in the cybersecurity industry since 2006, even though the parent company had been developing it since 1986. Let's look at the pros and cons below:

Pros

- You get robust antivirus protection against malware, viruses, ransomware, and other online threats with real-time scanning and detection to keep your system secure.
- Avira comes with various scanning options, for example, quick scan, full system scan, and custom scan, so you can choose the depth and focus of the scan based on your immediate needs.
- Avira can protect you from phishing attempts and malicious websites, ensuring a safer browsing experience.
- The free version provides essential protection just in case you do not require advanced features.
- Some versions of Avira include tools to protect you from identity theft and unauthorized access to your personal information.
- The paid version of Avira includes a firewall and optimization tools, enhancing security and improving system performance.
- Like Avast, Avira generally provides a user-friendly interface, making it easy for you to navigate and use the software.

Cons

- The free version of Avira may lack some advanced features available only in the paid versions, potentially limiting your security options unless you pay up.
- The free Avira might display occasional pop-up ads. The point here is to encourage an upgrade to the paid version, but ads can be quite intrusive.
- The VPN service provided in the free version of Avira has limited data usage, which may not be sufficient if you need access to a wider VPN range.
- In case you have any issues, customer support for the free version might be limited compared to the paid version, potentially leading to longer response times or fewer available support options.

The price starts at $34.99 for the first year, but you can still enjoy ample protection using the free version.

Download it from their official website https://www. avira.com/

AVG

Developed by AVG Technologies, this is one of the subsidiary companies owned by Avast.

Pros

- You get robust protection against a wide range of threats, effectively detecting and neutralizing malware.

- Given the multiple scanning options, you can customize your scans on a need basis.
- AVG includes features to secure online activities, protecting you from malicious websites and infected email attachments.
- Some versions of AVG come with tools to improve system performance by optimizing settings and removing unnecessary files, which can help speed up the performance of your devices.
- AVG offers tools to protect your privacy online and against identity theft.

Cons

- Depending on the kind of device you are using, AVG can be resource-intensive, potentially slowing down your system at times.

Price starts at $46.68 a year for each device, though you can also enjoy ample protection using the free version.

Download it from their official website https://www.avg.com/

Bitdefender

As a notoriously lightweight antivirus, Bitdefender packs quite a punch in the kind of protection you enjoy. The Romanian software company has been around since 2001.

Pros

- Bitdefender is highly regarded for its strong malware detection and removal capabilities.
- It is a lightweight antivirus, hence minimal impact on system performance, ensuring that devices run smoothly even during scans.
- Bitdefender offers a wide range of features, including advanced threat protection, privacy tools, VPN, and more in its premium versions.
- Bitdefender offers solutions for various operating systems, including Windows, macOS, Android, and iOS.

Cons

- Might be too expensive if you're getting licenses for multiple devices.
- The VPN service is not quite reliable, especially if you are a heavy user.

Price starts at $34.99 for the first year

Download it from their official website https://www. bitdefender.com/

ESET

The Slovak cybersecurity company has been around since 1992, with users in more than 200 countries.

Pros

- ESET comes highly regarded for its strong malware detection and removal capabilities. It provides reliable protection against viruses, ransomware, spyware, and other types of malware.
- ESET is relatively light on resource consumption, so it doesn't interfere with system performance.
- Despite the fast scanner capabilities, the thoroughness of the detection process is not compromised.
- ESET includes features to protect you from network-based attacks, ensuring a safer online experience.

Cons

- It gets costlier when you're signing up for multiple licenses.
- ESET's parental control features might be less comprehensive compared to some other antivirus solutions in the market, offering fewer options for monitoring and managing children's online activities.
- Their customer service isn't necessarily one of the most responsive, a concern that has been widely raised by lots of customers.

Price starts at $49.95 a year

Download it from their official website https://www.eset.com/

G DATA

Headquartered in Bochum, Germany, G Data's founders are widely recognized for creating the first antivirus software in the world. Moreso, G Data is also powered by two engines, a Bitdefender engine, and an in-house engine, offering unique scanning capabilities to both business and home users.

Pros

- G Data is known for its dual-engine antivirus technology, which combines two scanning engines to provide comprehensive protection against malware, viruses, ransomware, and other threats. This dual-engine approach aims to increase detection rates and reduce false positives.
- G Data typically boasts high malware detection rates, effectively identifying and removing threats from devices.
- Some versions of G Data include dedicated features for secure online banking and financial transactions, adding an extra layer of protection for sensitive activities.
- They also offer firewall and network protection features that help prevent unauthorized access to devices and protect against network-based threats.

Cons

- Some users might find the interface and settings of G Data's software relatively complex, especially for those less familiar with technical configurations.
- While the dual engine is great for security reasons, scanning might take longer compared to some other antivirus software, potentially affecting system performance during scans.
- They don't offer as many additional features compared to competitors, such as comprehensive optimization tools or privacy-related features.

The price starts at $29.95 in the first year for one device.

Download it from their official website https://www.gdatasoftware.com/

Malwarebytes

Founded in 2006, Malwarebytes is a multi-platform anti-malware software that's essentially a malware scanner. Compared to other antivirus programs in the market, Malwarebytes uses a batch scanning approach to limit interference with your performance, especially if you have more than one antivirus program running on your system.

Pros

- Malwarebytes is highly effective at detecting and removing various types of malware, including viruses, trojans, spyware, ransomware, and adware.
- You enjoy real-time protection, actively monitoring your system for threats and preventing malware infections before they can interfere with your system.
- Unlike other antivirus programs, you can use Malwarebytes alongside other antivirus software as an additional layer of protection, providing a specialized focus on malware detection and removal. This is useful because most antivirus programs detect competitor programs as malware, and suggest that you remove them.
- The browser security extensions can help prevent access to malicious websites and block intrusive ads.

Cons

- The free version is a bit cumbersome because you must manually scan your device. For real-time and scheduled scans, you must purchase the premium version.
- Malwarebytes is primarily an anti-malware solution, not a full-scale antivirus program. Thus, you cannot rely on it as your only security solution. You must use Malwarebytes alongside another antivirus program, making this a costly experience.

- While strong against malware, Malwarebytes might not offer the breadth of protection against other online threats that some full-scale antivirus suites provide.

Price starts at $3.75 per month

Download it from their official website https://www. malwarebytes.com/

McAfee

McAfee is one of the oldest antivirus solutions in the market, founded in 1987. If you are old enough to remember Windows 98 and Windows XP, you probably have used McAfee at some point.

Pros

- McAfee offers comprehensive protection against various threats including viruses, malware, ransomware, spyware, phishing attacks, and more.
- It provides solutions for different platforms including Windows, macOS, Android, and iOS, ensuring protection across multiple devices.
- McAfee provides identity protection features to safeguard personal information and prevent identity theft.

Cons

- McAfee has always been notoriously known as one of the most resource-intensive antivirus solutions in the market.

Price starts at $19.99 a year

Download it from their official website https://www. mcafee.com/

Microsoft Defender

The product was first available as an anti-spyware solution in Windows XP before it was later improved for later versions of Windows.

Pros

- It comes pre-installed and integrated into Windows 10 and later versions, offering basic protection without the need for additional downloads or installations.
- Microsoft Defender provides real-time scanning and protection against various malware threats, including viruses, ransomware, spyware, and other malicious software.
- The fact that it comes built-in gives you the advantage of running in the background with minimal interference on your system performance.

- Microsoft frequently releases updates and definition files to keep the antivirus software up-to-date, ensuring protection against the latest threats.
- Since it is already integrated into Windows, it's compatible with the operating system and generally straightforward to use, especially if you are the kind of user who does not wish to fiddle around with system settings.
- It is also integrated with the Microsoft Edge browser, offering protection against phishing attempts and malicious websites.

Cons

- It is quite a basic antivirus solution, and might not be reliable if you need advanced features, so you might have to download and pay for other commercial options.
- In independent tests, Microsoft Defender has sometimes shown lower detection rates against certain advanced and zero-day threats compared to other antivirus solutions.
- While it offers support for multiple operating systems including Android, Linux, iOS, and macOS, it does not support Windows versions older than Windows 7.

It is free for family and personal use, but for cloud services, the price starts at $5.11 a month.

Download it from their official website

https://www.microsoft.com/en-us/microsoft-365/microsoft-defender-for-individuals

Norton

Founded in 1990 and currently used by millions of users all over the world, Norton is known for providing all-in-one protection to users, making it an ideal solution for families and other home users.

Pros

- It is highly effective at detecting and removing malware, consistently ranking well in independent lab tests for its malware detection rates.
- Compared to competing products, Norton is considerably light on system resources.
- The user interface is quite intuitive, making it a darling among families and users with varying levels of technical skills.

Cons

- Norton has been known to flag legitimate software or files as potential threats, resulting in false positive detections.
- Norton's notifications and pop-ups, usually to remind you of pending scans or updates, are notoriously a nuisance among users.

- On rare occasions, Norton might have compatibility issues with certain software or cause conflicts on some systems.

Price starts at $59.99 for the first year, though they offer random discounts that could see you pay as low as $19.99 a year.

Download it from their official website https://us.norton.com/

Trend Micro

The Japanese cybersecurity outfit's attention is mainly on enterprise solutions, like cloud computing, endpoints, containers, servers, and enterprise network solutions.

Pros

- Given their focus on enterprise-level solutions, you enjoy robust protection against various types of malware.
- Trend Micro uses advanced AI and machine learning technologies to enhance its threat detection capabilities and identify new and evolving threats.
- It offers solutions for various operating systems, including Windows, macOS, Android, and iOS, ensuring compatibility across different devices.

Cons

- Some users may find the interface or settings somewhat complex, especially for users less familiar with technical configurations. This is primarily because of their emphasis on enterprise-level solutions.

Price starts at $19.95 a year

Download it from their official website

https://www.trendmicro.com/en_us/forHome/products/antivirus-plus.html

Each of the antivirus programs above provides firewall, email security, and protection against ransomware. If you are willing to pay more, you can have additional services like phishing protection, VPN, two-factor authentication, and anti-spam support, among other services unique to each product.

Ultimately, when you're choosing the right antivirus program for your devices, you should look not only at a solution that you can afford but also one that will keep your systems safe without straining your computing resources and slowing you down. The list above is a good place to start your search for the right antivirus solution.

For more information on internet security and how to protect yourself and your loved ones online, here are some insightful resources from the North Carolina Department of Justice.

Interactive Element

Q1. Why do you need an antivirus?

Antivirus software is essential for maintaining the security of devices and preventing cyber threats. They act as a crucial defense against malware and other threats that can compromise sensitive data, damage your systems, and steal personal information.

Q2. What does it mean to have safe browsing habits?

Safe browsing means behavior that minimizes the risk of encountering malicious threats or scams online. It includes being cautious about online activities and taking steps to protect personal information and devices.

Q3. How do you protect kids from online threats?

- Educate and communicate - Teach kids about online safety, including the dangers of sharing personal information, interacting with strangers, and recognizing potential risks.
- Monitor and guide them - Supervise their online activities, set boundaries on screen time, and guide them on safe and appropriate online behavior.
- Use parental controls - Use parental control features on devices and internet services to limit access to

inappropriate content and monitor their online activities.

Q4. How can I protect the elderly from cyber threats?

- Educate on scams - Teach them about common online scams, for example, phishing emails, fraudulent calls, and fake websites, and teach them how to identify and avoid these scams.
- Encourage skepticism: Encourage them to be cautious when sharing personal information online or responding to unsolicited requests for information or money.
- Use security settings: help them set up security features on their devices, including strong passwords, antivirus software, and enabling security updates.

Our world revolves around communication and most of that takes place online. How do you protect your emails and chats so they don't end up in the wrong hands? We dive into this in the next chapter.

6

Cybersecurity in Online Communication

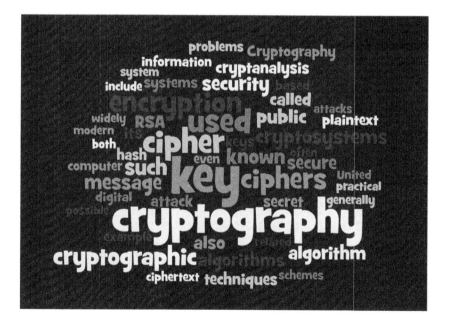

Birthdays are a good opportunity to celebrate the milestones you've accomplished in life. They are more than a reminder that each year comes with growth, but also a reminder that everyone and everything starts from somewhere. You are where you are today because, at some point in time, there was a humble beginning. The same can be said of communication.

Today, our world revolves around fast, efficient communication. You send and receive feedback in seconds. You can call and talk to someone in a different part of the world effortlessly, so much so that it almost feels like you are in the same space. But, communication wasn't always like that. If anything, communication has come a long way, from the ancient man, the early 15th Century to the instantaneous communication we have today.

Even though the earliest models of communication were quite rudimentary, and had loopholes strewn all over, that's not the case today. Communication models have advanced over the years in line with our desire for modernization and growing demands for efficiency. More importantly, as our society advanced, so did the value of communication. This explains why there's been a greater emphasis on enhancing privacy and security around engagements, just as much as the desire to get the message across as fast as possible.

In the age of information, the context and content of your engagements are more valuable than ever. You might not realize it, but the content of your communication could be valuable to some stranger, and unfortunately, you may never know why. From physical handwritten letters to email exchanges with your associates, cyber threats are real, so it's wise to assume that there's always someone in the shadows, trying to intercept your communication.

Given this harsh reality, you should be more alert with every form of communication you use, so that your engagement does not fall into the wrong hands. The point of this section is to explore different strategies to help you protect your engagements.

Protecting Your Emails

Emails are the lifeline of modern communication. Whether you're using them for personal or professional reasons, your email is an important part of your life. From a professional point of view, this is how you engage customers, your work-mates, or even for academic purposes. Similarly, your email is your gateway to different personal accounts, such as your Netflix account, your online shopping accounts, social media, and so on. Without an email account, you could easily be locked out of accessing crucial services today.

Given the prominence of emails in our lives, it makes sense to protect your email with the same zeal with which you protect your passwords. Unfortunately, email addresses were designed to be shared. This also makes them an easy target for cyber-criminals, because of the certainty in getting an audience.

Here's a quick overview of common email security threats you face from time to time:

- Spam - Unsolicited emails that are usually prime targets for phishing
- Malware delivery - Emails that either contain malware links, attachments, or redirect you to a website that infects your system.
- System takeover - These emails leak your login details to criminals, which they use to take over your system, one of the easiest ways of executing DDoS attacks.
- Business Email Compromise (BEC) - This is where an employee transfers money from the company account to a criminal's account. The employee acts on instructions from the criminal, who impersonates a top-level executive.
- Social engineering - Psychological manipulation approach where criminals coerce you to share sensitive information.
- Domain squatting - In this case, criminals piggyback on a reputable brand's popularity by registering a domain that almost resembles the authentic one. For example, while most people are used to Amazon.com, very few will notice the difference if you clone the Amazon platform and use a domain name like Amazonn.com.
- Ransomware - Criminals hold your business hostage, and the only way to gain access is by paying them off.
- Configuration Challenges - This could be an innocent mistake by your engineers. If your email servers are not configured properly, your communication with customers could fall into the wrong hands. Criminals might also find loopholes to exploit your system.

- Insider Threats - A disgruntled employee, or one who's spying for your competitor could also share confidential information.
- Weak security - Many people don't have strong passwords for their emails. Others use the same password across multiple accounts.

Looking at the risks above, email security should be a priority going forward, especially if you consider the kind of access and control that cyber hackers can have over you if they manage to swindle their way into your life. Here are some security measures you can put in place, both at a personal and professional level:

- Strong password - Well, this is as simple as it gets. Use as many characters in your password as possible, and avoid obvious password combinations.
- Use proxies - This keeps your internet activity safe and private.
- Learning - Make an effort to learn about email security. It's easier to protect yourself against something you know than what you don't know.
- Gateway email content filter - They scan incoming emails for malware or any other malicious script that could leave you vulnerable.
- Two-factor authentication (2FA) - An extra layer of protection in case someone leaks your password.
- Anti-Phishing Solutions - There are lots of anti-phishing solutions in the market, including your

antivirus programs which flag and reduce your
exposure to phishing attempts.

- Encrypt all connections and communication to ensure
it's only accessible to the intended parties.
- Update your antivirus and email solutions regularly so
you have the latest security patches.

Finally, remember that even though these solutions are effective, they will not always work 100%. Besides, criminals keep upgrading and reinventing their methods to have a better shot at taking advantage of you. Bearing that in mind, you must always remain vigilant, and if something seems too good to be true, it probably is.

Instant Messaging Apps and Programs

WhatsApp, Viber, Telegram, Messenger, WeChat, LINE, Adium, Bitbee, and Jitsi are some of the most popular instant messaging platforms today. They've been around for years, going through different security upgrades and changes in that time. Whichever of these you use, is a matter of personal preference. Have you ever stopped to wonder how they handle security, and whether your data on these platforms is as secure as they promise you?

Instant messaging remains an important part of modern communication, hence the need to prioritize security while at it. Whether you're using the messengers for personal or professional reasons, you should be aware of the potential risks, and how to work around them. Here are some common security threats affecting instant messaging services that you should be aware of:

- Virus and Worms - There's been an influx of such attacks on instant messaging platforms since 2014, with some of the most devastating attacks making the list of top infections across all devices.
- Identity theft/authentication spoofing - Anonymous identities are so easy to create. Most people have pseudo accounts for different reasons, not necessarily for criminal purposes. The problem comes in when such accounts are used for malicious reasons.
- Firewall tunneling - Instant messaging apps can be quite risky depending on how you connect to the internet. For example, if your app connects through random ports or peer-to-peer connections, there's always a risk of exploitation, especially if you're using a platform that isn't end-to-end encrypted.
- Data security leaks - A lot of companies ban the use of instant messaging apps within the business premises because they don't have control over them. Without this, there's always a risk of people sharing privileged information, and since there's no audit trail, it's not easy to hold them accountable for their actions.
- Spim - This is spam but for instant messaging platforms. You've probably come across such content before. They are just as disruptive as email spam, but given the nature of instant messaging services, they spread faster, and have a wider reach because of the element of trust between the person sharing it and the

recipients. The intention, however, remains the same, phishing and data pilferage.

People usually assume that security threats only exist on emails and the websites they access. However, the fact is that anything that can connect to the internet has a fair chance of being a security exploit. Besides, the assumption that instant messenger solutions are somewhat free from exploitation means that you lower your guard, and that's how criminals get their way in.

Going by the potential risks we've outlined above, you must be careful when choosing the right instant messaging solution, either for personal use or for your business. Here are some important security features you should consider when selecting an appropriate instant messaging solution:

- Encryption - This is a given. Encryption is one of those must-haves that you should never compromise on. Your data must always be safe from prying eyes.
- Data hosting - Choose a platform that hosts their data on-premise. A lot of companies are moving away from cloud solutions to providing the same services directly to their clients, simply so they have more control over their data protection and security needs.
- Two-factor authentication - This, like end-to-end encryption, is another feature you should never compromise on. We'll not go into detail as we've discussed it at length throughout the book.
- App integration - Consider the permissions you must share with your favorite messaging apps, especially if

you wish to integrate them with third-party apps for enhanced functionality.

- Regulatory compliance - What regulatory standards apply in your jurisdiction? More importantly, does the messaging platform abide by those standards? Have they ever had a run-in with the authorities over regulatory malpractice?
- Simplicity - An ideal messaging platform should have an interface so simple that you can install and use it seamlessly. If you have to train people to use it, the training process should not be complicated.
- Open source code - One good thing about open source code is that there's a lot of room for improvement. As long as the messaging app's code is publicly available, there's an active community of developers who are always coming up with suggestions on how to make the product better, safer, and more inclusive.

Note that while all the features above are good to have, they might not always be available on all the platforms all the time. Therefore, at times the best choice comes down to a balance of convenience and security, or in a nutshell, deciding what you can overlook or give up, but have measures in place to mitigate the potential risks that might arise as a result of that compromise.

The #1 Best Practice: End-to-End Encryption

If you use WhatsApp Messenger, you might be familiar with the image below. You'll see it especially when you start a conversation with a new number.

What is end-to-end encryption, and why is it important?

Ideally, what companies like WhatsApp are telling you is that your data is safe with them. More importantly, they are promising you that no one can access your data from their servers, neither themselves nor any other third party. So, other than yourself and the person you are communicating with, the only way someone could access your conversation is to physically gain access to your device.

Encryption simply means scrambling your information in a manner that makes it so unreadable that if it ever fell into the wrong hands, it would be useless to them. An encrypted message can only be deciphered by the sender and recipient because it requires a special cryptographic key only available to those two. Anyone else who intercepts that message will not be able to decrypt it because they don't have the key.

End-to-end encryption is a unique type of encryption that keeps your data encrypted at every point. For example, if you send a text message on WhatsApp, it is encrypted right when it leaves your phone, and will still be encrypted at the destination.

This is important in that it eliminates the popular man-in-the-middle hacks, where someone could intercept your message from whatever server is used to relay it. Therefore, whether the message has been received or not, it remains safely encrypted, so no one can access it, not even your internet service provider (ISP). Other entities that could overreach their mandate and intercept your communication like your network administrator, or even the government can no longer legally do that anymore, thanks to end-to-end encryption. I've added "legally" here especially where the government is involved. In dire circumstances, say when national security is at stake, the government has been known to go to insane lengths to try and break the encryption protocols. It's quite a lengthy and resource-intensive process, and since the outcome might not even be guaranteed, it's not worth the trouble, for anyone else who doesn't have the kind of resources the government has.

So, how does end-to-end encryption work?

Say you want to chat with a customer privately. On your end, you'll have two keys, private and public. These are the crypto-graphic keys we mentioned earlier. Your public key can be shared with anyone, but your private key is personal, and you are the only one who should be able to access it.

Your public key encrypts the message when you hit send, so no one other than the customer can read it. This message will be processed through different servers between yours and your customer's phone. None of these servers can decrypt the message because they don't have the cryptographic key.

When the message gets to your customer, they will decrypt it with their private key, because it is a personal message meant for their eyes only. The same process is repeated when the customer responds and throughout the conversation.

End-to-end encryption is a smart way to protect your communication online at a time when our privacy online comes under threat from different angles. Here are some of the advantages:

- There's a lower risk of third parties intercepting your communication.
- Without your private keys, it's almost impossible to interpret your unencrypted data.
- Protects your data from tampering, which is quite useful in this age of fake news.
- Your private conversations remain private

There are different methods of implementing end-to-end encryption on your systems. However, given the complexity involved, the best option is to use services that automatically have the encryption protocols enabled.

Don't Phish for Trouble

At times trouble finds you, but in some cases, you go looking for trouble. That's how phishing works. Phishing happens when a criminal tries to bait you with something you might like, or something that will get your attention. More often phishing scams impersonate companies or businesses you are familiar with, and tempt you into sharing personal information with the criminals.

Phishing is one of the social engineering tactics criminals use to prey on you. It's psychological warfare at best because they'll try to coerce you, create an element of fear or urgency so you can act fast and give them what they need. By the time you realize the mistake you've made, they'll have all the information they need to execute a full-scale attack.

When you click a link on the phishing mail, you're redirected to a fake website where you'll provide the information they ask you, usually by filling out a form that seems authentic. People have become aware of this trick, so it doesn't always work. As a result, criminals went a step higher, and instead of redirecting you to their fake website to harvest your information, they prompt you to download an attachment. Well, even though you might not have given them the information they need, the attachment on your device is loaded with malware that installs and runs stealthily as soon as you open it.

A popular phishing scam that many people still fall for today is one where you get an email claiming that you've won a lottery, and need to provide your bank account and contact details so they wire the money into your account. They'd also ask you to send a small fee to help them process your winnings. In such a case, the criminals are preying on your greed, because why would you get excited about winning a lottery you never even subscribed to in the first place?

There are lots of other phishing scams, and most of them follow the same approach, trying to lure you with the promise of some too-good-to-be-true return. Here are some common phishing characteristics that should get your alarm bells ringing:

- You get an email claiming suspicious log-in attempts or activity on an account you might not even have—do not click on that link!
- You receive a notice that your payment information is not correct, or there's a problem with your account so you should fill out a form to update your information—it's a trap. If it's an account you recognize, like your bank account, call the bank or better yet, visit the bank in person.
- They send you an invoice for a transaction you don't recognize and ask you to clarify some information on it. It's probably a fake, and they need your payment information.
- Do not click on any link to make payments, especially for accounts or businesses you've never interacted with before. At this point, I'd assume you know what your frequent online account purchases look like, whether

it's Amazon, eBay, or any other, you're quite familiar with their payment process.

- If you receive a notification that you are eligible for some refund, usually a government refund you have to register, it's a fake.

As you can see above, the fact that phishing emails usually resemble official emails means that you must be careful each time you receive an official email. For example, before you engage an email from UPS or BestBuy, check the sender's address to make sure it's legitimate. Legitimate emails generally don't ask you to click on links, so it's probably a phishing attempt.

There are lots of reliable resources from which you can learn about safe online communication, and how to protect yourself from scammers, and phishing attempts. Here's a good example from the FBI.

Interactive Element

Q1. What's the role of cybersecurity in communication?

To ensure that sensitive information exchanged through various channels remains confidential, and available only to authorized parties. It helps prevent data breaches, unauthorized access, and interception of confidential conversations or messages.

Q2. Can you name some measures you can take to protect online communication?

- End-to-end encryption ensures that messages are encrypted from the sender's device and can only be decrypted by the intended recipient.
- Engage over secure communication protocols and channels like HTTPS for web browsing to transmit data securely.
- Use encryption to encode messages and make them unreadable to anyone without the decryption key.
- Use VPN tunnels for secure data transmission over public networks.

Q3: How do you avoid phishing attacks?

- Always verify the sender's email address and check for spelling errors or unusual requests in your email.
- Do not click on suspicious links. Hover over them to see the actual URL destination before clicking.
- Confirm any urgent or unusual requests that seem rushed through a different communication method (call or visit the official office if possible directly) before taking action.
- Enable two-factor authentication to prevent unauthorized access even if your passwords are compromised.
- Keep learning about phishing tactics and regularly update your cybersecurity knowledge to recognize and avoid potential attacks.

Sending and receiving emails isn't the only form of communication. Sending and receiving money, and payment for goods or services, in a way, are also a form of communication. They communicate satisfaction hence the customer's willingness to pay. Having discussed how to keep your engagements safe online, let's now explore the dynamics of protecting your money online.

7

Wallet on The Web; Securing Digital Financial Transactions

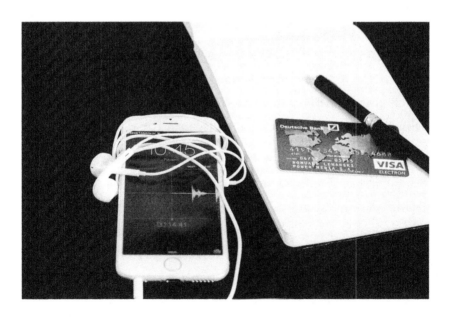

If we're ever to assess the impact of the growth and evolution of the digital world, one of the best examples would be the world of finance, especially if we cast our gaze on globalization. Digital finance evolves in response to growing and dynamic market demands. Today, we are in the age of cryptocurrency, with many proponents optimistic about the era of mass adoption, especially in light of the upcoming Bitcoin halving event. This is but the tip of the iceberg. Have you ever wondered how we got here?

The transformation in the digital financial sector seems to happen so fast, but that's just proof of how dynamic the digital world is. If you conduct a deep analysis of all the events that have taken place in a year, it might feel like you're talking about five or ten years worth of transformation. An important takeaway from this is the need to be more proactive in securing your digital financial ecosystem. Given the lightning pace at which things evolve, the last thing you want to do is be left behind as the digital financial landscape evolves.

As the world of finance evolves, so does our approach to money management. Features like contactless payment platforms, cryptocurrencies, mobile wallets, and online banking were unfathomable some years back, yet today, they are the very foundation upon which digital finance thrives. These features have been a success because they offer one thing that we all crave—convenience!

It's quite empowering when you think about it. It takes you seconds to send someone money across continents, without having to visit your bank. People are conducting business across borders, shipping goods worth billions of dollars on the high seas, and all this is possible without physically going to the bank. Such is the beauty of convenience.

But, convenience does come with its unique risks. Criminals understand that convenience breeds comfort, and therein lies their opportunity to exploit you. They constantly seek opportunities to exploit vulnerabilities in the digital infrastructure, and unfortunately, at times we usher them in through the front door without even realizing it.

While the evolution in digital finance has made life easier, it's also brought about unique risks, hence the need to be proactive in securing your digital financial landscape. For every technological advancement you embrace in digital finance, you must similarly implement appropriate robust security measures to safeguard your interests.

In this chapter, we'll explore two crucial aspects of online security: how to protect your banking and shopping activities online. To navigate this landscape safely, you don't necessarily need to understand the complexities of online security. Instead, we will delve into simple, yet effective measures you can implement right away. Remember, you're not just protecting yourself, but your entire household.

According to the Federal Trade Commission (FTC), criminals made away with more than $8 billion in 2022. Most of this was through fraudulent investments, fake business and job opportunities, fake lottery claims, identity fraud, imposters, and exploiting vulnerabilities in online shopping platforms. While the stats are alarming, the worst of it all is that this was a 30% increase in crime from the previous year.

An industry that experiences a 30% year-on-year growth must be quite a thriving one, right? It's alarming because the growth of cybercrime is happening at a time when globally, we're dealing with a lot of struggles. Some industries are yet to fully recover from the impact of COVID-19, the recession, inflationary pressures, and the spillover effects of the war in Ukraine, yet proceeds from cybercrime have gone up by 30%. What this means is that criminals are getting smarter and more proactive at finding ways to exploit you, hence the need for you to fervently fight back.

Growth of Online Transactions and The Associated Risks

Even though convenience in the digital ecosystem has its unique risks, we cannot ignore how easy it has made life, and in particular, business. Online businesses continue to enjoy tremendous growth, recording massive strides each year. Today, almost all businesses have an online footprint. Both customers and business owners understand the inherent benefits of engaging online, and more importantly, the fact that there's something in it for everyone. Business owners have a market as wide as their imagination, while customers enjoy the benefit of variety, without having to physically walk into every shop to compare prices.

You can get almost everything you need online today. Whether you're looking for physical goods, digital products, or services, you'll always find someone online who has what you need. It gets even better, some traders can deliver right to your doorstep instantly…and they don't even have the financial muscle that giants like Amazon have. The digital ecosystem has spurred creativity among entrepreneurs, which in the long run, works well for customers.

In 2019, online stores only accounted for around 14% of global retail sales. Five years later, this has grown to 22%, proving the massive growth potential in online retail. If we factor in some of the developments that have taken place in recent times, like mass adoption of cryptocurrency, growth in dropshipping, and the fact that a lot of people are currently embracing the gig economy or setting up side hustles online, digital retail is poised for tremendous growth over the next five years. Amazon, for example, was responsible for more than 39% of retail commerce sales in the US for 2022. To put this into perspective, for every $5 spent online in the US in 2022, $2 went to Amazon.

The Flip Side of the E-Commerce Boom

Growth in digital commerce is amazing. It champions our entrepreneurial spirit, pushing us to seek innovative solutions for immediate problems. Unfortunately, cybercriminals also lurk behind the scenes, waiting to exploit unsuspecting users. Here are some common criminal activities you should be aware of, which have plagued the online business community:

- Adware - These are random ads that pop up on your screen. While some adware could be running to earn the website owner some revenue, cybercriminals can also use them to infect your system or trick you into a fraudulent website that collects your information.
- Data breaches - Cyber criminals are always trying to hack credit card companies, banks, and retailers to access your personal and financial information, which could then be used to directly hack your accounts and steal your money.
- Fake online stores - Criminals clone popular websites or set up fake e-commerce platforms, complete with logos and brand themes that seem legitimate at first glance. If you buy from them, you either receive counterfeit products or in some cases, they take your money and block your contacts.
- Identity theft - In this case, criminals try to hack common e-commerce platforms to obtain your payment and login details. They either sell your information on the dark web or impersonate you and use your payment information for their purchases.
- Phishing - Hackers send you an email that at first glance, looks like it comes from a genuine sender. For example, the email could look like it came from Amazon, but if you scrutinize the sender's information, you realize it's a fake. Most of these emails either encourage you to click on a link or download the attached document, either of which will initiate a malware attack that steals your data.

- Unencrypted data - Learn to be mindful of the kind of websites you access. Some websites are not encrypted, so any information you share through them could be accessible to hackers. Examples are websites whose SSL certificates are not updated and websites that begin with HTTP instead of HTTPS.

Going by the risks above, you must be more intentional in protecting your online activities from criminals. Even though some website owners put measures in place to protect their users, you cannot always rely on their goodwill. When it comes to online security, you are your first line of defense. Never forget that.

The Technological Evolution of Banking and Finance

There has been tremendous growth in e-commerce over the years. While most of this growth can be attributed to evolving customer demands and business models, the banking and finance sectors have played a crucial role by providing the appropriate supporting infrastructure.

Even though e-commerce has been on a steady growth trajectory, the COVID-19 pandemic changed everything. The global movement restrictions meant that people had to find alternative ways of getting by, and this played right into the growth narrative for e-commerce. Since then, businesses with digital outlets have thrived while some brick-and-mortar outlets have either had to reinvent themselves online or close shop altogether.

By bringing services like insurance, credit, and payments online, the financial sector has completely embedded itself into the fabric of e-commerce, providing timely solutions across the board for both individuals and companies. More importantly, this business model has also benefited businesses in the financial sector through increased efficiency, and reduced overheads, making it easier for them to maximize revenue.

Financial technology (Fintech) and e-commerce go hand in hand. Both sectors bring convenience to businesses and customers by streamlining business processes and making them trustworthy, convenient, and efficient. Features like payment processors and online banking support the need for seamless and secure business transactions, two things that customers and business owners appreciate in online business.

According to a 2021 report by the World Bank, more than 75% of the global adult population owns an account with a financial institution. This is impressive, especially when compared to 68% in 2017, and 51% in 2011. Similarly, more than two-thirds of the global adult population conduct digital payments today.

With more businesses coming online, the utility value of digital payments becomes more apparent. New business opportunities sprung up since the COVID-19 pandemic, hence the need for wider financial inclusion. The beauty of digital payments is that they don't just make business processes easier, they also widen access. Digital payments allow users in underbanked communities to enjoy the same access to financial services as those who have access to banks and other financial institutions.

Similar to the discussion we had earlier on potential personal risks you face online, the banking and finance sector is not immune to criminal activities either. Below are some criminal activities that plague this sector, and threaten to derail the progress achieved so far:

- Theft of banking information
- Fraud
- Identity theft
- Money laundering

One of the biggest challenges with the crimes in this sector is that it's a high-risk-high-reward business. Criminals understand this and invest heavily in some of the latest software, systems, and technology to support their nefarious agenda.

Even though players in the financial sector like banks and third-party service providers like PayPal are also making significant strides towards protecting their customers through know your customer (KYC), anti-money laundering, and various counter-fraud mechanisms, at the end of the day, you should always be aware of the potential threats around you.

Safe Online Shopping

Given what you now know about online security, it's clear that you must take bold measures to protect yourself online. Criminals are always lurking around, so here are some simple tips you can implement for a safer online shopping experience:

- Research the company or seller - As a rule of thumb, find out as much information as possible about the online seller or company before you buy from them, or share your information with them.
- Use secure payment methods - There are lots of secure payment solutions available online, which offer various protections for both buyers and sellers. Use escrows where possible, but more importantly, be wary of anyone who insists on direct payment to their bank accounts.

- Keep a record of every transaction - You'd rather have this information but not need it than need it and not have it. For every transaction you make online, keep a record of important details like the price, product description, order number, and receipt.

- Shop only on secure sites - Make sure you're accessing a website with the right security measures in place. By default, a secure website must start with https. If you only see http without the "s", then that platform does not encrypt your data, so walk away.

- Update your e-commerce software - You cannot actively protect yourself from all the malware and criminal activities online. That's where software developers come in. They regularly release updates to mitigate the latest threats in the market, so all you have to do is update your software and you'll be good to go.

- Use strong passwords - Stop using easy-to-remember passwords like birthdays, your names, or anything that has admin. Beef up your security with strong passwords. If you don't know how to begin, get a password manager to generate a strong password for you. More importantly, do not use the same password on multiple accounts.

- Don't click on links - Never click on links in your emails, especially emails from people you don't know. This could also apply to emails from people you know, who might have been compromised without their knowledge. In particular, be suspicious of links that promise you outrageous deals.

- Put devices on lockdown - Sign out of all accounts you use online as soon as you are done shopping. Many websites offer to save your payment information for a seamless experience the next time you want to shop with them. Do not allow them to remember your information. It's safer to go through the lengthy process of keying in your details each time.

- Outsmart email scams - There's nothing special about the "special offers" you keep getting in your email. Most of them are links to malware, or phishing attempts. Don't open emails from people you don't know, and if you receive an email that's supposedly from your bank, call your account manager to confirm if it's authentic before you act on it.

- Skip optional fields - When entering your information on a website, only provide what's necessary. Skip anything that's marked as optional. For example, some websites will ask for three names, but only the first and last ones are mandatory. In this case, you don't need to give them your middle name.

- Use secure networks - Avoid public networks and free internet hotspots. Whether you're at the airport, or in your favorite restaurant, do not use their networks. If you need to use your laptop online, set up a hotspot on your phone instead.

- Pay with credit, not debit - Credit cards are generally safer for online purchases than debit cards. If someone hacks your debit card, they'll have access to all the money in your account. Your credit card, on the other hand, probably has a $0 fraud liability clause, protecting you in case your card details are compromised.

Secure Online Banking

Online banking is fast and convenient. Criminals also enjoy the same benefits. They can wipe you clean just as fast as you can pay for stuff online. Here are some simple tips to protect your online banking activities:

- Choose strong and unique passwords - Similar to our point on online shopping above, stop using simple, easy-to-remember passwords. Use a password generator to set unique, and complex passwords, and never use the same password on more than one account.
- Enable two-factor authentication (2FA) - If this option is available, use it. 2FA adds an extra layer of protection just in case someone happens to know your password. They cannot access your account without the authentication code.
- Steer clear of public Wi-Fi - Avoid these like the plague. It doesn't matter how urgent your transaction is, the risks are far greater. Criminals only need a few seconds, but the impact of their actions could affect the rest of your life.
- Sign up for banking alerts - Opt-in for alerts via text message or email for any transaction on your account. This makes it easier to identify a transaction you did not authorize and alert your bank right away. You can

also get alerts for changes to your personal information, failed login attempts, new accounts linked to your existing accounts, and balance limit alerts.

- Be wary of phishing scams - Criminals send these by email or text message, pretending to be from your bank. They'll either install malware on your system to monitor your keystrokes or send you to a dummy website where you'll give them all the information they need to wipe your accounts clean.
- Do not share your details with anyone - Personal information is private for a reason. Do not share them with anyone, not even your friends or family members. If, for example, you have to share some information with your partner, make sure they understand the security measures you put in place.
- Do not use public computers to log in - Never sign into your accounts from public computers. Only use your phone or laptop. The same applies to a friend's phone, laptop, or PC. You never know whether their devices are compromised or not. This is a rule you should enforce strictly.
- Choose trustworthy financial apps - The fintech sector is currently awash with financial apps. Avoid apps that link to your bank accounts, for example, budgeting apps. If you must install a banking app, make sure it's the official app from your bank, and download it from the official app store, or your bank's website.
- Regularly check online bank savings accounts - Monitor your accounts frequently to make sure your balances are correct, and alert your bank to investigate

any erroneous entries. Do not ignore even the slightest error on your accounts.

Finally, online security is a constantly evolving matter, so it's in your best interest to refresh your knowledge from time to time and keep up with the changing trends. The Consumer Finance Protection Bureau (CFPB) is one reliable resource that can come in handy.

Interactive Element

Q1. Why is E-Commerce security important?

To protect sensitive information, such as credit card details, personal data, and financial transactions, conducted online. It ensures that customer information is protected from unauthorized access, fraud, and data breaches.

Q2. How do criminals exploit your online banking accounts?

Criminals use different methods, but the most common ones are as follows:

- They infect devices with malware through downloads or compromised websites, allowing them to steal login details or hijack your banking sessions.
- Sending deceptive emails or messages that appear legitimate, tricking you into revealing login credentials or clicking on malicious links (phishing).

- Manipulating you into divulging sensitive information or granting access through tactics like impersonation or fake support calls (social engineering).

Q3. How can I ensure the security of online transactions?

- Always have two-factor authentication enabled on your accounts, especially those linked to online transactions.
- Always use secure websites with HTTPS and a padlock icon in the address bar, indicating encrypted connections.
- Keep an eye on your bank statements and account activity to detect any unauthorized transactions promptly.
- Never use public networks. However urgent you feel the transaction is, do not engage on public Wi-Fi networks or unsecured connections.
- Verify vendor authenticity and only engage reputable sellers and validate the legitimacy of the website or platform before making a purchase.

Whether it's shopping or online banking, the security of your digital wallet is something you cannot take for granted. The key takeaway from this section is that technology evolves, so do cybersecurity threats, and so must your vigilance around your money. Next, we look at how to stay safe in a world that's increasingly going mobile.

8

On-The-Go Security for Mobile Devices

O ur world gets increasingly interconnected by the day. From economies to populations and shared cultures, everything is available at the flick of a screen, or touch of a button. That's the beauty of globalization, and the internet is right at the heart of it all. With this interconnectivity, however, also comes the ease of criminal exploits. Mobile device usage is on the rise. From flagship feature phones to tablets and wearable devices, there's a whole lot of mobile technology that we interact with every day. While these devices make life easier in different capacities, they also are an easier route into our lives, and criminals will always try to capitalize on that.

In this chapter, we will explore how to secure your digital assets, especially in mobile gadgets like tablets and phones, because these are some of the most commonly targeted devices by cybercriminals. It doesn't matter where you are, or the kind of device model you use, you must keep your device safe.

The Internet of Things (IoT): A Threatscape Analysis

The Internet of Things (IoT) isn't just another buzzword. It's a networked concept of heterogeneous devices that interact with each other, without direct human or human-computer intervention. This kind of networking hinges on the use of sensors that enable the seamless interaction between devices. You can have anything from self-driving cars to home appliances connect and exchange data independently.

While IoT is an exciting concept, it also comes with unique challenges, mostly as a result of the innate vulnerabilities in each of the devices that are connected to the network. On top of that, the mobility of some of the devices also creates room for possible attacks at different levels. This is one of the biggest risks in IoT, it's not easy to preempt the particular point of vulnerability due to the heterogeneity of the member devices.

We could argue that hacking an IoT network is quite easy because all a criminal needs to do is figure out vulnerabilities in any of the devices on the network. This creates a problem because IoT devices have been deployed in many sectors, from medical devices to industrial control systems and smart homes. Take your home, for example. You could have a robust security system, but the smart thermostat in your living room could be the loophole that a criminal exploits. It's important, therefore, that you understand the vulnerabilities of each device you onboard in your IoT network, and figure out how to mitigate potential risks.

IoT attacks are relatively different from normal attacks in the tech sector, simply because of the multiplicity of possible vulnerability points. For this reason, you'd have to consider additional measures to protect the devices on your IoT network. Here are some differences you might notice between an IoT attack and a normal tech attack.

- **Legacy Problems**

With IoT, the emphasis is mostly on the utility you get from the devices, and not necessarily the network aspect. For example, you buy a smart refrigerator so it can give you more than 10 years of good service. Once it's on the network, you'll probably forget about it, and only access it remotely when you need to.

The problem with such devices is that their long lifespan increases the risk of using an obsolete security system. Say five or ten years down the line, as long as the refrigerator is working, you'll be satisfied. You might not realize that the security software on it is obsolete. After all, its core function is to preserve your food, not internet connectivity.

Now, on the flip side, you are more informed about security updates on something like your router, or laptop. You could easily upgrade your router or laptop for the latest and most secure model in the market, something you cannot do for your smart refrigerator.

- **Threat Impact Assessment**

Most tech attacks are aimed at service disruption, stealing data, cyberbullying, and so on. More often, the aim is to interfere with the target's mode of operation. While the attacks could be a nuisance and create an unknown level of loss, the recovery process is relatively straightforward.

On the other hand, IoT networks support crucial devices and infrastructure, for example, in hospitals. A successful attack on such a network could have far-reaching effects, including loss of life.

- **Device and Network Complexity**

The structure and design of IoT networks vary from one user to the next. Your smart home network, for example, is not the same as the IoT network running in the local hospital. Given such differences, it's not easy to create a one-size-fits-all approach to securing the networks. As a result, some networks could enjoy better security than others running the same security apparatus, leaving room for security exploits.

On the other hand, security patches for normal IT attacks can be deployed seamlessly and serve a wide range of needs. At times all it takes is to update your antivirus with the latest patch on all your devices and you're good to go.

Protecting IoT Devices

Growth in IoT is similar to growth in the use of AI. Both concepts exist at a time when interest in cybersecurity is at an all-time high, and for a good reason. Most of our lives are currently online, so it's only fair that you take appropriate steps to protect the digital ecosystem. The number of potential threats continues to grow as more people integrate these concepts into their lives. From wearable devices to tablets, smartphones, and devices in your smart home network, it's easier to protect your IoT network when you are aware of the vulnerabilities you might be exposed to. Here are common IoT risks you should be aware of:

- Vulnerability in the form of unencrypted data, weak passwords, or using outdated software.
- Risk of privacy breaches, since most of the devices collect a lot of data on your usage patterns and behavior.
- Inability to create standard security apparatus because each device on an IoT network could be running a unique security system.
- Susceptibility to botnet attacks. A botnet is an elaborate criminal-controlled network made up of infected devices, commonly used to deploy DDoS attacks.
- Some device weaknesses could be a result of manufacturer defects which you might not be aware of. Such devices are compromised even before you buy them. Adding such devices to your IoT network increases your risk exposure.
- Some IoT devices rarely receive security patches or updates, making them easy pickings for criminals.
- If your devices have weak authorization and authentication processes, criminals can easily exploit them. Once they gain access, you cannot tell what else they could do on your network.

Despite the multiple weak points in IoT devices, you can still take proactive steps to protect your network and the devices on it. The precautionary measures are quite simple, and in most cases, approaches you've already used before on other security systems. Here are some simple tips you should explore:

- Disable unnecessary features, for example, not all smart devices need to be online.
- Ensure your software is always updated.
- Change default credentials like admin and root usernames.
- Segment your network in a manner such that you have dedicated network access for different tasks. You can have a guest network, smart devices network, and so on. This way, vulnerabilities on the IoT network are isolated from other networks.
- Invest in intrusion detection systems, and antivirus, and use the right firewall solutions.
- Use strong encryption solutions.
- Keep the devices on your network invisible, making it harder for anyone on the network to identify and exploit their vulnerabilities.
- Enable two-factor authentication.
- Restrict network access.

The solutions above are a good starting point, but the most important thing in online security is usually to stay vigilant at all times. Remember, the more IoT devices running on your network, the greater your potential threat exposure.

Mobile vs. PC: The Security Debate

Which is the most secure between your mobile phone and your PC? This is a never-ending debate you come across each year, especially in the aftermath of a widespread hack on either of the devices. While there are valid arguments in favor of the security of each of these devices, it's not usually a fair comparison given the environments within which they operate. On top of that, each device can only be secure to the extent of the user's behavior. For example, you could own one of the most secure devices ever, but if you constantly visit piracy networks, there's a good chance you'll expose yourself to hackers.

Compared to PCs, mobile devices leave you exposed to more risks because of their convenience value. Think about it for a moment, with your phone, everything you need online is always a few seconds away. You might even risk using that free Wi-Fi hotspot occasionally. The fact that you are always on the move also brings you within a proximate distance of different kinds of attackers.

Most apps on your mobile devices demand GPS location access, without which, you cannot use the apps. That alone means that someone's always tracking your every move. These apps don't just track your location, they also send comprehensive reports. This means that you are not only vulnerable if someone hacks your phone, but you might also be at risk in the event of a hack on the developer's side.

Other than mobility, there's greater risk in mobile devices because a successful exploit could give a hacker access to your entire life. Think about it for a moment. If someone gains control of your phone, they will have your messages, photos, emails, videos, contacts, browser history, and location history. It doesn't take much after that, to figure your entire life out.

Besides, smartphones are great for social engineering exploits. Given the ease with which we share files within our trusted circles, all a hacker needs to do is get into your device and you'll give them access to your inner circle. We could argue from a hacker's point of view, therefore, that there are greater returns in hacking mobile devices than PCs, given the wider target audience.

That being said, whichever of mobiles and PCs are riskier than the other will always come down to user behavior. From a manufacturer or developer's point of view, neither of the devices can be said to be better or less protected than the other. Let's explore the possible security concerns across these devices, so you can make an informed decision on this.

- **On Privacy**

Google estimates that 7% of desktop websites are infected with malware every month. This means that you are often exposed to spyware, trojans, spyware, and adware. While this might sound alarming, did you know that 3% of Android devices come with malware preinstalled by the developers? 3% might seem an insignificant amount until you consider the number of Android devices in the market.

• On Infection

Building on the fact that some apps come preloaded with malware, the Android dev ecosystem tends to be less conscious about security than iOS. If you frequently visit third-party app markets other than Google's Play Store, your risks are even greater.

This risk is lower in PCs because in most cases, you could simply reinstall your operating system and start afresh. Besides, if a program comes preloaded with malware, most antivirus solutions can easily detect the infection.

• On Security

Criminals understand that hacking your mobile device gives them easier access to your inner circle, so they are more motivated to exploit mobile devices than PCs.

Looking at the three points above, whichever of the two you prefer is a personal choice. When it comes to security, however, it's up to you to decide the kind of digital lifestyle you live. If you visit risky platforms all the time, your risks will always be higher than what most people are exposed to.

Mobile Security: App-Based Measures for Device Protection

The future is mobile. From remote work to business and even studying, mobile brings the kind of convenience that truly makes life easier. Since you can access everything you need easily, mobile devices will always be a target for criminals. Whichever mobile device you prefer to use, whether it's a wearable device, tablet, or smartphone, it's important to protect your digital lifestyle. Here are some simple security features usually built into most mobile devices that you can use:

- **Lock Screen**

Lock your screen as soon as your phone is idle. It might seem like an inconvenience when you need to use the device, but that's a small price to pay for security. You can even set the lock screen pattern to be invisible, making it harder for someone to guess your unlock pattern.

- **Voice Control**

Voice control is a security feature where the device can only respond to commands from your voice. Even though it became popular on personal assistants like Alexa, Siri, and Google Assistant, it's become a common feature on many mobile devices today, as long as they have voice recognition built-in.

- **Software Updates**

Make sure you update your software frequently. You cannot individually protect your devices against all the threats online, so this is an easier alternative. At some point, you might also need to consider upgrading your hardware, because there comes a time when you cannot update the software beyond some point. This is common in mobile operating systems. Android and iOS devices, for example, only support a select number of devices with their latest software updates. Older models become obsolete over time, and can no longer receive the latest security updates.

- **Two-factor authentication (2FA)**

Enable two-factor authentication on any device, program, or app where the feature is available. It gives you an added layer of protection whenever your password is required. 2FA is not limited to security codes you receive on your phone or email.

In some cases, authentication could be through biometrics like voice or facial recognition.

- **Find my Phone**

This is a simple security feature that helps you remotely track your phone if you lose it. You can also lock or erase data on the phone remotely. If it's online, you can see the wireless network it's connected to.

- **Phone Identification**

Write down the unique identifiers for your phone and save them elsewhere. These can come in handy when you report a stolen device to the police. Find your IMEI code, for example, by keying in *#06#.

- **Data Encryption**

It's quite simple. Encrypt your phone data, especially if you use cloud backup solutions like Google Drive and Dropbox. Encryption makes it harder for hackers to extract and make use of your data if you ever lose your phone. Do the same for your laptops and any other data-handling device you own.

- **Password Protection**

Keep all the important apps on your phone under password protection. From your banking apps, to chat and photo apps, anything that you feel is important should always be password protected. This makes it harder for someone to access them if they steal your phone.

To get the best out of mobile security, you must strike a healthy balance between the convenience you desire, and the safety protocols you need. Take the lock screen feature, for example. While it might seem tedious to unlock your screen each time you need to use your phone, it's a simple security feature that protects your device from prying eyes, and more importantly, from access by unauthorized users. If you ever lose your phone, someone would have to figure out how to unlock your pattern, code, or password. If that's not possible, their only solution would be to wipe the device clean, which prevents your data from falling into the wrong hands.

At the same time, get into the habit of going beyond the ordinary. Many people just use phones and apps without taking the time to read the privacy policies, terms, and conditions of use. While the legal jargon seems like too much work, they exist for a reason. You need to understand, for example, how your data will be used, and the remedies available to you in case your data is ever exposed by a problem from the developer's end.

Unfortunately, there's not much you can do about the privacy policies, terms, and conditions. More often, you can either accept them and use the platform, or reject them and not use the platform. You do, however, have a choice in what the apps on your phone can access. All you have to do is go to your phone settings, identify the app, and manage the permissions.

Why is this important?

Well, some permissions are on by default, but you can turn them off, and turn them on when you need to use the app. Ideally, you should only allow app permissions when necessary. For example, let's say you don't like the basic calculator app that comes preinstalled on your phone, and instead, you download one from the app store. It makes no sense for a calculator app to require access to your location, camera, contacts, or read your texts. Uninstall that app, because it's collecting information about you that doesn't match its core functions. If you still insist on using the app, turn off those permissions.

Mobile devices today are not just smart, they are also designed to be intelligent. When someone gains access to your device, they essentially have front-row seats to every aspect of your personal and professional life, your contacts, and finances. This is why you should always prioritize security over convenience. The few steps you take to secure your mobile devices are worth so much more if you consider what's at stake.

For more information on how to protect your mobile devices, here's some useful insight from the Cybersecurity & Infrastructure Security Agency (CISA)

Interactive Element

Q1. Why should you be concerned about IoT security?

IoT devices, while convenient, can be vulnerable to cyber attacks due to their interconnected nature. Ensuring their security is crucial to prevent potential risks.

Q2. How do I protect my IoT network?

- Always monitor IoT devices for any unusual behavior or signs of compromise.
- Change default passwords and reconfigure security settings on IoT devices.
- Create a separate network for IoT devices to isolate them from sensitive data and critical systems.
- Use strong encryption methods to protect data transmitted between devices and networks.
- Where possible, keep devices updated with the latest firmware and security patches to fix vulnerabilities.

Q3. What steps can I take to boost mobile security?

- Install antivirus and anti-malware apps to scan and detect malicious software, protecting your mobile devices from malware infections.
- Encrypt internet connections with reliable VPN apps, especially when using public Wi-Fi (I highly discourage this) or accessing sensitive information.

- Use password managers to store and generate strong, unique passwords for different accounts, enhancing overall security.
- Use browsers with enhanced security, for example, unique privacy features, block malicious sites and prevent tracking.

The question of which is the most secure between your mobile and desktop computers is one that we might never convincingly answer, because it comes down to perspective, and how you use your devices. However, what's certain is that there are relevant security measures for each of these devices, and you should implement them. With that knowledge, we now turn our attention to your home. How can you keep your home network and devices connected to it safe? Well, let's find out in the next chapter.

9

Defending Your Home Network

Hirow secure is your home network?

It's quite funny, that a lot of people recognize the effort their employers put into securing the company networks, but when they get back home, they throw all caution to the wind. This laxity usually comes from the assumption that our homes are safe from cyberattacks. This, unfortunately, is not the case. If anything, weak or lack of security in home networks has proven quite a challenge for many companies. This is because instead of working hard to penetrate the fortress of a security network in the company, all a criminal has to do is trail someone to their homes, sneak into their devices, and wait to be transferred into the company through the front door. It might seem far-fetched, like an idea out of a movie, but it's as real as it gets.

We take home security for granted, yet our homes should be the safest place we know. Since the COVID-19 pandemic, a lot of people started working remotely, bringing home security into the spotlight. Most homes today also double up as remote working stations, so even though there isn't much that your employer can do about security in your home, you must take the initiative and protect your home networks. Any vulnerabilities on your end could have far-reaching effects on your employer, and might even cost you your job.

Cyber threats around your home network can threaten not just your job, but also disrupt the peace of mind you expect to enjoy at home. Once a criminal is inside your home network, you can never predict what they'll do, or who they'll go after. It could be your kids, your friends who visit from time to time, or even your parents. One thing that's certain about cyber attacks is that they always target the most vulnerable, so you cannot take chances with your home network security anymore.

Securing your home network should be as serious as the alarm systems you have in place to protect your home from burglaries. If anything, the stakes are much higher with network security, because a criminal that penetrates your network can easily access your contacts, photos, videos, online bank accounts, addresses, and even install spyware and remotely record what's happening in your home.

Virtual Vulnerabilities at Home

Whether you're working from home or not, the modern home is incomplete without an internet connection. You probably have a smart TV, and a few other gadgets at home that require a steady internet connection, so it makes sense to have internet at home. If anything, the internet today is pretty much a basic need, high up on the list of priorities together with food, shelter, and clothing.

You'll need Wi-Fi for convenience, making it easier to access the internet from anywhere in the house. A good wireless router can help with this, so all your devices from your smart TV to your phones, tablets, printers, and any other IoT device can all be online.

Decent routers can provide reliable coverage across a 100-feet radius. However, if you notice network blindspots, you might need to get a range extender. Network blind spots mean there are some parts of the house where you either get a low internet connection or none at all. This could be because the positioning of doors and walls in your house blocks the network signal, or your house might be too big for a single wireless router.

Once your router is set up, you can either keep a single network or create multiple networks on the router depending on your needs. For example, if you have a dedicated office space at home, you can create an office network separate from the network that serves your smart TV and everywhere else. This way, your bandwidth is apportioned in a way that heavy usage in the living room will not interfere with your webinar or any other office tasks.

Looking at the dynamic nature of internet usage at home, network security is a crucial part of your home network. Set a strong password for your router, just like you do for your email and other accounts. Though it might not always be necessary, you can also create a wireless name that's difficult to guess.

The image below shows how easy it is for a hacker to exploit your home once they have a way in.

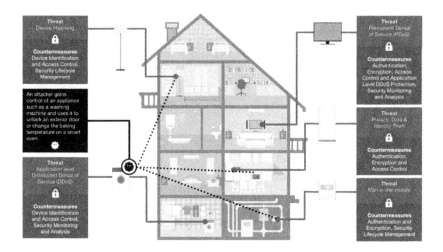

Visualization adapted from (Rambus, 2023)

Here are the password conventions that you can consider to secure your home network:

- Wi-Fi Protected Access Version 2 (WPA2) - This is the recommended standard for most wireless networks and is more secure than the predecessors, WPA and WEP.
- WPA3 - Has been around since 2018, and was designed to address some of the security flaws around WPA2, with an emphasis on both client and router-side encryption. You can think of this as end-to-end encryption. One thing you can also appreciate about WPA3 is that the encryption is dynamic, changing from time to time, so if someone somehow gains access to your network, their connection will only remain active

in that session, and they'll be kicked out as soon as they terminate that session.

- Using Media Access Control (MAC) addresses - Every device has a MAC address. In this case, you set up your wireless network such that the only devices that can access the network are those whose MAC addresses are bound to it. Therefore, even if you have the wireless password, as long as the MAC address of your device is not on the accepted list, you'll never access the internet on that wireless network. While this might be effective, someone could simply copy a MAC address for one of the devices on the network, gain access, and even lock out everyone else.

Whichever of these options you choose is a matter of preference. Note, however, that you must still be vigilant about your network security as you are about your email passwords. It's also good practice to change the network name and password from time to time.

How Does Home WiFi Become Unsafe?

Despite the security measures we've outlined above, your home network might still be vulnerable. There are two possible points of entry that hackers exploit to infiltrate your network; weak IoT devices, or vulnerabilities in your network. There's not much you can do about IoT devices, because some of their vulnerabilities come from the supply side. The best you can do is to strengthen your network security to try and limit exposure due to the manufacturer's defaults.

On the other hand, you are in control and should make some smart decisions about your local network. Common vulnerabilities that hackers exploit include are as follows:

- Weak network names like admin, home network, and root.
- Weak encryption protocols, for example, you're still using WEP or WPA.
- Weak network passwords.
- Not changing the default access credentials set by the manufacturer.

If you're using weak encryption protocols or credentials, it takes a hacker just a few minutes to breach your network. All they have to do is intercept data packets in transmission and use brute force to decode it.

Other than the two broad categories above, here are some common security threats that hackers exploit and infiltrate your home network:

- DoS attacks - This is where hackers disrupt your network by flooding too many requests that it can handle, effectively taking you offline.
- Eavesdropping - In this case, hackers monitor your network activity and lay in wait for sensitive information like payment information, login credentials, or other personal details. This is also the tactic used in Man-in-the-middle exploits.

- Evil twin attack - Hackers essentially clone your network. Since you can't immediately tell which is the correct one, you might access the fake network, giving them access to everything.
- Malware and viruses - All a hacker has to do is infect one device on your network, and use it as ground zero, to infect and take over every other device that comes online.
- Physical attacks - In this case, the hackers gain physical access to your router, either by breaking into your home or any other possible option, and reconfigure it in a manner that compromises your security. The problem with this kind of attack is that you might never know if you've been exposed because everything usually works normally.
- Social engineering - In this case, criminals try to trick or scare you into giving them privileged information either by calling you and running the scam, or sending you malicious emails.
- Unauthorized access - If you're using weak passwords or default manufacturer passwords, you'll always be a target. Criminals are always monitoring networks for poorly protected networks and devices. You'll also be exposed if you're still using WEP and WPS encryptions.

The suggestions above give you better insight into network vulnerabilities, and more importantly, some of the things you should be on the lookout for to build a secure and robust home network.

Common Home Devices' Level of Potential Threat

Unlike your workplace where your network administrators can easily identify foreign devices, or identify the source of a threat from an audit trail, most home users cannot explain the possible origin of a threat, simply because we have too many devices connected to the home network, and they might not even own some of those devices.

You might not have all of them in your home but know that your threat exposure increases with each device you introduce to your home network. So, how do these devices make your network vulnerable?

First, each of the devices in your home has a unique architecture, with vulnerabilities that you might not know about. Hackers who know about the vulnerabilities in, for example, certain DVR and baby monitor models, will simply search for their IP addresses online and try to gain access to the networks they belong to. This approach is common for autonomous devices that don't require user interaction. All you have to do is connect the device to your network and probably plug it into a power source and it will run non-stop.

Given the ever-evolving threat landscape, non-technical users do not have the skills to protect their home networks appropriately. Even tech-savvy users have fallen victim to some of the simplest security exploits before, which only proves that when it comes to home network security, we take a lot for granted.

The graph below shows a list of common devices in our homes, and their level of threat risk:

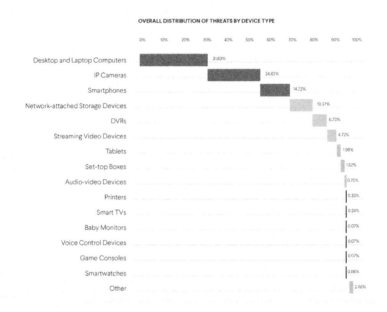

OVERALL DISTRIBUTION OF THREATS BY DEVICE TYPE

Device	Percentage
Desktop and Laptop Computers	31.63%
IP Cameras	24.63%
Smartphones	14.22%
Network-attached Storage Devices	10.37%
DVRs	6.73%
Streaming Video Devices	4.72%
Tablets	1.98%
Set-top Boxes	1.52%
Audio-video Devices	0.70%
Printers	0.33%
Smart TVs	0.24%
Baby Monitors	0.07%
Voice Control Devices	0.07%
Game Consoles	0.07%
Smartwatches	0.06%
Other	2.46%

Visualization adapted from (Vos, 2023)

Here are some key reasons why hackers have an easier time exploiting your home network through the devices in your home:

- Most consumers simply don't go the extra mile to secure their networks. Some don't have the technical know-how, while others simply don't care.
- Manufacturers are limited by resources, or the need to capitalize on profitability, so they focus on the product's core functions and ignore networking flaws.

- Some devices automatically alter your network settings for ease of interoperability, especially to enhance their functionality when used across multiple devices. Unfortunately, this leaves you exposed.
- Some devices run outdated operating systems, or systems with weak security protocols, and since they won't get security patches or updates, they could be the loopholes hackers use to target you.
- Your internet service providers (ISPs) are not bothered to go the extra mile. While there are a lot of threats that could be prevented from the ISP's side given their caretaker role in your networks, many ISPs approach this as an added or premium service, so you have to pay more for better protection, which most home users cannot.

At the end of the day, your network security is your responsibility. As the world gets more connected, a lot more devices come online, especially at home. Some of these devices come with configurations that could conflict with others on your network. The best option for you is not just investing in robust security, but also to try and learn some of the network capabilities and vulnerabilities inherent to each device you bring home. This could help you preempt possible intrusions, and prevent hackers from taking over your home network.

So, how safe is your wireless network?

Take the simple Wi-Fi security test in the Interactive section at the end of this chapter to find out.

Setting up a Secure Home Network

Looking at the potential threats around you, it's logical to wonder how you can protect yourself against all that. The thing about network security is that it always comes down to a personal initiative. For example, given your knowledge of the rigid security measures in your workplace, you can choose to take similar measures to protect your home network. Besides, the more devices connected to your network, the higher your security exposure, so it only makes sense that you know how to protect your network. Here are some simple security tips to get you started:

- Limit exposure by setting your router in a central spot in the house. Other than a strong signal, you also reduce the risks of signal pilferage outside your home.
- Password security is paramount. Don't just choose a strong password for your network, make sure you change it as frequently as possible.
- Do not use the default router login credentials. Change them as soon as your network is configured and ready to go.
- Firewalls and Wi-Fi encryption are generally available on routers, but it's wise to confirm if they are active than to assume.
- To avoid sharing your network password, create a guest network. Change the password as often as possible, or as soon as your guests leave.
- If you're connecting to a public network, use a VPN to obscure your internet footprint.

- Always update your devices and your router. Get the latest version of your router if possible, as there's a good chance it has better security measures than the one you have. To be precise, get yourself a WPA3 router.

- Never allow remote router access. Turn it off, because it allows anyone who's connected to your network to change the router settings. Someone could easily lock you out.

- Check the devices connected to your network to ensure they are familiar devices. If you notice a strange device, kick it out instantly and change all your network settings.

- If you're not at home, it's always wise to turn off your router. After all, no one is using it anyway.

- Set up parental controls to limit the duration of time your kids stay online.

- Go to the advanced settings on your router to monitor network traffic. From this setting, you can view and set limits for incoming and outgoing traffic.

- Implement a network security monitor (NSM) and an intrusion detection system (IDS) to help you detect potential threats.

- Use a Pi-hole (sinkhole/blackhole) to protect your network. Essentially, it intercepts DNS queries on your network and verifies them against blocked, flagged, or malicious domains. The Pi-hole effectively blocks any domain that's on the unwanted list.

Finally, network security will always come down to the choices you make. Even with the strongest network settings so far, the idea of 100% security is impossible. As long as cybercriminals exist, they'll always come up with smarter ways of exploiting network security vulnerabilities. Your best bet is to stay vigilant and keep learning about advancements and innovations in network security.

For more information on how to protect your home network, here's some useful insight from the National Security Agency (NSA).

Interactive Element

Q1. How would you define home network security?

This means protecting all devices that connect to the internet within your household from cyber threats.

Q2. Why is home network security important?

To protect personal data, privacy, and devices from cyber threats. A secure home network prevents unauthorized access, malware infections, data breaches, and potential hacking attempts on connected devices, ensuring a safer online experience for everyone in the household.

Q3. What can I do to make my home network more secure?

- Device security - Keep all devices updated with the latest security patches and antivirus software.
- Firewall - Enable the router's built-in firewall to block unauthorized access to the network.
- Network encryption - Use WPA3 encryption for Wi-Fi and avoid using WEP or other outdated security protocols.
- Router security - Update router firmware regularly and change default admin passwords.
- Strong passwords: Use strong and unique passwords for the Wi-Fi network and devices.

Use the following resources to help you assess your network security:

https://www.secjuice.com/wifi-security-testing-handbook-getting-started-2/

https://www.linkedin.com/pulse/free-resources-wifi-security-pentesting-mejbaur-bahar-fagun/

Most people aren't as concerned about network security at home as they are in their workplaces. This is an unfortunate scenario, given the number of devices that connect to our home networks, and the risks that we are exposed to as a result. The fact that most people don't secure their home networks doesn't mean that you shouldn't either. This is your wake-up call, so make a bold move and be more proactive about network security at home. Since there's so much we can learn about a robust security network from the workplace, let's explore cybersecurity in the workplace and see if we can borrow a leaf from the corporate approach.

10

Cybersecurity in the Workplace

These are exciting times. There was a time when remote working was the preserve of a few companies that most of us would envy. We'd think of them as revolutionaries in the employment sector, employers who cared deeply for their staff, so much that they allowed them to work from the comfort of their homes and pop into the office a few times a week...until COVID-19 happened!

The pandemic forced the entire global workforce to rethink the entire workforce dynamic. First, we had widespread lockdowns where everything pretty much ground to a halt. Then everyone realized that we were going to be stuck in the lockdowns for an unknown duration, so we had to figure things out and figure them out fast. That's when remote working became a thing. It wasn't just about a few revolutionary companies anymore, it became a way of life.

As time evolved beyond the pandemic, many companies fully embraced remote working models, while some adopted hybrid models. Online work was once something we'd mostly associate with freelancers. Today, online work is the ideal business model. For employees, you get a semblance of work-life balance, so you don't have to miss out on important milestones in your household while stuck in traffic. For employers, there are lots of cost savings involved, and since employees appreciate the flexibility of having both their professional and personal lives running concurrently, they are happier.

Employers and employees are not the only ones excited about online work, cybercriminals are too. If anything, they've always been working remotely, so none of this is new to them. If you can recall, in the earlier days of the COVID-19 pandemic, criminals would hack into Zoom calls for various companies and cause all manner of chaos. This proves that they have well been ahead of the pack, and with the majority of the global workforce coming online, things just got juicier for the average cybercriminal.

While the rise of online work has been a godsend for many people, it's also given rise to a flurry of cyber attacks that threaten to disrupt what should have been a harmonious digital workspace. If you're taking your business online or planning to do so soon, you must have an elaborate cybersecurity plan, otherwise, you could easily become the latest in a long list of victims of cybercrime.

Remote work is amazing. At times you wonder whether the world would be a better place if we embraced remote work a few years earlier. Think about it for a moment, the number of people who have struggled with work-related stress over the years would probably be lower since more people would be able to work and still spend as much time as possible with their loved ones. However, remote work also poses significant security risks.

In the workplace, you have elaborate security measures in place. You could even describe your work setup as a unique ecosystem. For example, some companies don't allow foreign devices onto their networks, and this includes employee smartphones. You probably can't even use a USB drive on the company computers, so if you ever wish to share or transfer files, you must do it over the company network, leaving an auditable trail.

Now, when we move the workforce online, and have people working from their homes, such security measures do not apply anymore. Employers have no control over what their staff do in their homes, the devices they access, and so on. This is where cybercriminals take advantage, and why cybersecurity is such an important discussion right now.

Given the dynamic and constantly advancing threats in digital workspaces, it would be wise to establish clear security protocols and procedures, particularly for remote working models where employers cannot exercise full control over their employees' digital lifestyles. There's got to be a way of protecting the organization's data integrity without necessarily intruding or imposing on the remote employee, so a win-win situation for everyone.

While there are several ways to go about this, the industry-wide consensus is that the only way we can uphold and strengthen cybersecurity is if everyone involved makes it their initiative. They say the weakest point in any security apparatus is usually the human element. You can build the most robust, impenetrable security system in the world, but all that effort could be undone by a simple human error, for example, someone was in a hurry and forgot to log out, or went online to watch the Super Bowl and clicked on an ad. It's usually the mundane things we don't read much into that allow criminals a way into the inner sanctum of our security systems.

Therefore, when it comes to strengthening security around the digital workspace, we have to think beyond policy and procedure. We must build an all-inclusive security apparatus where remote workers have a sense of ownership. Instead of pushing down security instructions, make remote workers a part of the solution. Involve them in discussing and mitigating evolving threats around them, engage them on suggestions to map the way forward, and so on. It's not just about engaging on the way forward but having a remote workforce that shares the same commitment to online security as the organization does.

Work and Cybersecurity

One of the biggest misconceptions in the digital space is that criminals are only interested in big companies. Well, penetrating an entity like Microsoft has its perks, and you could make a lot of money, but it would similarly cost a criminal quite a fortune to even make it to the front porch. So, why bother?

Instead of going after the big fish, criminals come after easier prey, small businesses. Most small businesses don't take security seriously, and that's why they become easy pickings for anyone, from beginners to experienced hackers. Many small business owners generally don't think they are big enough to be worthy of an attack like that's something to be proud of. Criminals, on the other hand, prey on this inferiority complex.

While you might think of yourself as "just a small business", here are some reasons why criminals look at you and see a cash cow:

- You could be using some amazing intellectual property, for example, your source code, that's probably worth a lot more than you've realized.
- You process lots of financial data, so anyone who can gain access to your architecture could be smiling all the way to yours and their bank.
- You hold customer payment records and information.
- You process sensitive information for customers, including their addresses, contacts, Social Security details, and so on.
- You run some powerful computer systems, so criminals could be interested in piggybacking on your computing resources.
- Well, you're a business after all, so you do have some cash lying around, which a criminal would be interested in diverting.

Come to think about it, while criminals could be dissuaded from attacking a massive entity like Microsoft, your weak security could be their way in. Many small businesses buy enterprise solutions from big companies. It could be anything from supply chain management to information sharing and management solutions. If a criminal penetrates your security system, that's how they gain access to the presumably difficult-to-hack larger entities. As you can see, your small business isn't that small after all, and you must take security seriously.

Common entry points for criminals into your business include ransomware, phishing, malware, data theft, threats from insider action, and social engineering. We covered these in Chapter 3, so we won't dive into that. The most important thing, therefore, is that you take security seriously. In the digital age, no business is too small to attract a hacker. As long as you are online, you'll always be valuable to someone, for something.

Given the imminent threats against your business, here's a three-step approach to help mitigate the risks and protect yourself:

Step 1: Embrace a Security Culture

You could have all the tools in place to protect your business, but if security is not built into your organizational culture, all that would be futile. Your people need to understand the risks involved, and why their security is crucial to everyone. Help them realize that there's more to this than the security protocols, so they can approach security from a bigger-picture perspective.

How do you achieve that?

Well, that occasional meeting or discussion on cybersecurity won't do. Security is an ongoing process, so you should have regular discussions, training, meet-ups, and anything else that can support your security initiatives. Encourage your team members to be proactive, especially in reporting anything that might seem out of place, or a mistake.

Step 2: Strategy

Create a long-term security strategy that involves security audits, policies, tools, and regular assessments to ensure your systems are at par with prevailing security standards. The point here is to gain oversight on all aspects of your security apparatus and ensure compliance with both internal and external security requirements.

An elaborate technical strategy, for example, could include any of the following:

- An intrusion detection system.
- Log manager.
- Content delivery network to mitigate DDoS attacks.
- Robust firewalls.
- Password generators and weak password detection alerts.
- Security reporting dashboard.

Even with these in place, you must still be vigilant, because even though most of them don't report breaches for different reasons, even the biggest, most secure businesses get attacked from time to time. Criminals innovate and come up with new tricks all the time, so you must similarly invest in a holistic approach to cybersecurity.

Step 3: It's About the People

We mentioned this briefly at the beginning of this chapter, which also ties into the first point on culture above. Security is about the people. Criminals will penetrate your system through your people. For that reason, you must build awareness into your business model to ensure your staff are trained, knowledgeable, and understand their role in cybersecurity. In cybersecurity, human error costs companies millions if not billions of dollars each year, so the best long-term approach is to encourage your people to be a part of the solution, or they will be the source of your problems.

Consequences of Neglecting Cybersecurity in the Workplace

Whether it's a remote, small, or large enterprise, you cannot afford to take cybersecurity for granted anymore. Criminals innovate all the time, so online threats are equally becoming more sophisticated, hence the need to take cybersecurity seriously. Given the brazen nature of cybercriminals, you can never really tell what their end goal is, when they come after you. Here's a brief overview of the possible risks of ignoring cybersecurity in the workplace:

- **Financial Loss**

Every security breach usually has a financial consequence, whether immediate or not. The problem is that you might not be able to tell the exact extent of the financial damage. Think about losing trade secrets, proprietary information, intellectual property, or sensitive customer data. Other than the immediate loss, you could still be sued by the victims, for example, your customers, for irresponsible data management protocols that left them exposed to criminal activities.

- **Breach of Trust**

Existing and prospective customers tend to avoid you as soon as they realize you've been hacked. Such incidents create a public outcry, which can damage your reputation, especially in the social media age where news travels so fast. As a result, you could lose a lot of business opportunities and have to spend so much more to remedy the situation.

- **Operational Loss**

The fact that someone has unwarranted access to your business operations means that in some capacity, you must slow down or stop your process altogether. Such a disruption can be catastrophic, depending on the nature of your business. You'll certainly miss some deadlines, misplaced deliveries, and some money will end up in the wrong hands. Such a disruption could take a while to resolve, during which you'll still be losing money. Other than that, it's not easy to convince your customers that you've completely dealt with the intrusion, so winning their trust back might be an uphill task.

- **Legal Challenges**

Businesses owe a legal responsibility to the people and entities they interact with. This means everyone from your employees to customers and business partners. You have a legal responsibility to process and manage their data responsibly, or as required by law. Governments all over the world have been enforcing data privacy and protection measures to ensure that all businesses are held accountable for the data they handle. As the custodian, you are responsible for safeguarding the integrity of data processed through your business. In the event of a breach, therefore, you could face dire legal consequences, which usually include fines heavy enough that they could cripple your entire operation.

At the end of the day, every criminal is unique. You might notice the criminal's immediate target, but that doesn't mean it's the only reason why they tried to exploit you. If anything, anyone who gains privileged access to your systems can cause harm on multiple fronts, hence the need to beef up your security apparatus. It's also worth a reminder that you don't just stand to lose data, but also business and other opportunities.

Response, Remedy, and Recovery

Security is one thing you can never take for granted. It doesn't matter whether you're a small business owner, or if you're approaching this from a corporate point of view, you must not just protect yourself online but also have preemptive measures in place to mitigate the risk of an attack. Anyone could get hacked at any given time, so for that reason, you must always be prepared.

We all believe, and at times, rightly so, that we have a robust security system in place. While that might be true, ask yourself one question—what happens if I'm hacked? It's quite a scary thought, but a possibility you'd be well-suited to prepare adequately for.

The biggest challenge for most people isn't usually being hacked, but what comes next. How do you pick yourself up from the intrusion? How do you engage your customers? What do you tell your customers and what information do you with-hold from them? How do you engage authorities? Will the hackers do it again? Even worse, have they gone, or are they still lurking around?

A security breach often leaves you with more questions than answers, and dwelling on that will only set you back further. A smart approach would be creating an elaborate response and recovery plan that helps you get back on your feet right away. Let's now explore a simple six-phase approach to response and recovery in the event of an attack:

Phase 1: Preparation

This is the most important phase of your response plan, one that never ends. Since no one can predict when they'll be attacked, you must always be prepared and assume that it could happen at any time. As a perpetually ongoing process, preparation involves the following:

- Training your team to ensure they know what to do in the event of a breach. The point here is to avoid panic since everyone knows what to do.
- Investing the right resources into protecting your business. This includes software solutions, the right hardware, and regular training sessions.
- Document and regularly review your mitigation strategy to ensure preparedness.
- Conducting random security drills to evaluate the effectiveness of your security measures.

The core objective of this phase is to avoid being blindsided and running into panic mode if you're ever attacked. The more prepared you are, the easier it gets to contain the situation and limit the damage.

Phase 2: Identify the Problem

If you've been hacked, you need as much detail as possible of the incident. This information will be useful, especially if you bring in external support to help you solve the problem. Here are some important issues you should address in this phase:

- What happened?
- What parts of the business have been affected?
- How was the incident discovered, when, and by whom?
- What's happened to the business since the incident was first reported?

Please note that at this point, no question is ever irrelevant or too small to make a difference. The more detailed your assessment, the easier it is to map the way forward.

Phase 3: Containment Measures

From your responses to the questions in Phase 2 above, you have some insight into the nature of the attack and the extent of the damage so far. The next step is to act on that information. How do you contain the situation and prevent the damage from spreading?

At this point, most people think that they can stop the rot by deleting everything. Unfortunately, such a knee-jerk reaction only creates more chaos, because once you lose all data, you can never truly investigate the breach, so you don't have any information to prop up your defenses for future reference.

Instead of deleting everything, think about containment. For example, take some, or in some instances, all devices offline. Before you do that, put out a notice for your customers so they do not panic. Remember, you might be able to control the situation in the company, but not what your customers do. A short-term approach could be letting your customers know that you're conducting a routine maintenance audit, and your systems will be back online as soon as your process is done. More importantly, you should have a redundancy plan in place, which could involve restoring one of your backups to run temporarily in a sandbox setup, so your business isn't fully crippled.

When someone gains illegal access to your business, it's wise to assume that access credentials have been compromised. Thus, it makes sense to revoke and renew access credentials across all levels when this is done.

Phase 4: Eradicate The Problem

Given what you already know about the breach, you can now figure out the root cause of the problem. You understand the kind of breach, the origin, the nature of the attack, and so on. There's a good chance that you're not the first business to suffer this attack, so you probably already know how other businesses handled their situation.

Whether it's a malware attack, DDoS, or whatever other problem, you can now viciously attack it from its root cause and eradicate it. Patch your systems, apply the most recent updates, and do anything necessary to rid your business of the problem. Do not take any chances. Be as thorough as possible, to ensure that when this is done, you can confidently bring your business back online.

Phase 5: Recovery and Restoration

Having got rid of the problem, start the recovery process. The point here is to assure your customers of the same confidence you have in your business. It's about getting your business running at full scale once again. You must also put measures in place to preempt a similar attack and prevent it from interrupting your operations.

Phase 6: Incident Review

At the end of every breach, you must take stock of what happened. While attacks are unfortunate and create a lot of problems, they are also vital learning opportunities that can help you strengthen your security apparatus and get better at preempting similar or advanced breaches in the future.

This is also a good opportunity to review the effectiveness of your response plan. Assess the measures that worked, and discard or improve those that failed. Preparedness drills can only get you so far. Your response to an attack, however, gives you real-life experience, and valuable lessons across the board.

As you can see above, the six-phase plan is quite straightforward and can be implemented across different business levels. However, you can still customize it to suit the complexity of your business. There isn't a single business owner alive who would wish to experience the horrors of an attack on their business. However, it's essential to have a plan in place, just in case someone's ever bold enough to come after you.

Security Best Practices

Beyond the six-phase plan we outlined above, you should also encourage your team members, especially those who work remotely, to implement simple practices that could help enhance their security at a personal level. More often, we focus on the potential threats at an organization-wide level and ignore the fact that at times, criminal elements can walk right through the front door, camouflaged in employee devices. Therefore, since it might not be possible to implement the six-phase mitigation approach in your employees' homes or over their devices, the best you can do is to champion responsible device usage.

Here are some simple strategies you can suggest to your employees:

- Encourage them to use updated antivirus solutions, and where possible, VPN services.
- Advise them to strictly avoid using their work devices for personal use.
- Work devices should never be accessed by, or used by family members. Enforce strict access credentials for this.

- Where possible, install a sliding camera cover over their computers and shut them when they are not using the cameras.
- Advise them on how to secure their wireless networks at home, including the use of strong passwords and password managers.
- Regularly train them and share literature on common scams, especially those targeting remote workers, for example, email scams.
- Keep the software on their devices regularly updated, and report any issues they might experience after an update.
- Encourage the use of multifactor authentication to strengthen their digital security.

If your team isn't working remotely, here are some additional measures to supplement the six-phase disaster mitigation strategy, which you can implement in the office:

- Conduct regular cybersecurity drills and audits.
- Enforce strict policies on the use of personal devices on the company network, or to access company files, commonly known as bring your own device (BYOD) policy.
- Ensure an auditable trail for accessing company files, which makes it easier to assess the situation in the event of a security breach.
- Make sure your teleconferencing solutions feature end-to-end encryption.

- Communicate policy changes and adjustments to your team in advance, with elaborate reasons so that they understand why the company is taking a step in a certain direction, and how it affects them.

Online work has grown over the years, whether remotely or in the office, most of the work we do revolves around the internet. As long as we work online, you must always have measures in place to mitigate and ward off potential threats when they happen. More importantly, you should have a disaster preparedness strategy to get back on your feet in the unfortunate event that your systems are exploited.

Here's a useful guideline from the National Initiative for Cybersecurity Careers, and Studies (NICCS), on setting up an elaborate cybersecurity framework to protect your work environment.

Interactive Element

Q1. What's your role in supporting the cybersecurity efforts in your place of work?

- Attend all training sessions to learn how to identify and respond to potential threats.
- Set strong and unique passwords for accounts and change them regularly.
- Report suspicious activity to the relevant IT/security teams as soon as you notice them.

- Strictly adhere to company policies on data handling, accessing sensitive information, and using company devices and networks securely.
- Keep devices, software, and applications updated with the latest security patches and antivirus software.

Q2. What are the potential consequences of ignoring cyber-security guidelines at work?

- Data breaches result in exposure or theft of company resources.
- Financial losses from theft, fraud, or disruptions to business operations caused by cyber-attacks.
- Loss of trust and credibility among customers, clients, or partners due to compromised security.
- Legal consequences like fines, penalties, or legal action for failing to protect sensitive information, especially if it involves regulatory compliance violations.

Q3. Why is it important for companies to establish, implement, and enforce cybersecurity measures in the workplace?

- Building a foundation for sustainable business growth by establishing a secure environment for operations.
- Enhancing productivity and efficiency by preventing system downtime due to cyber attacks.
- Ensuring compliance with industry regulations and data protection laws.
- Minimizing the risk of financial losses, data breaches, and reputational damage.

Life after the COVID-19 pandemic has been unpredictable at best, but it's also tested our resolve as a society. Our resolve to work hard and rise against adversity has been the hallmark of our excellence and resilience throughout history, and the pandemic was no different. From it, came remote work. Remote work is no longer the preserve of freelancers, but something that many companies have already embraced in the corporate sector. While it can be enjoyable, it also comes with unique challenges that hopefully, you are now well-equipped to handle. Finally, let's wrap things up with a discussion on back-ups, your ultimate digital lifeline when all else fails. Better safe than sorry, right?

11

Digital Lifeline: Data Backup and Recovery

If there's one thing I've learned throughout my career in cybersecurity, and which I've mentioned throughout this book, it's the fact that you are your first line of defense. When it comes to security online, website and app owners may or may not have appropriate security measures in place. Therefore, it's up to you to take precautionary measures to protect yourself. At the end of the day, no one understands the value of your data more than you do, hence the need to have a resolute Plan B.

The point of having a fallback plan is to mitigate against the risk of the worst possible scenarios. For example, let's say you've been hacked, or your systems are infected by malware or any other kind of virus, rendering them irrecoverable. What steps do you take from there?

Ideally, when it comes to online security, you need to think like a corporate entity. Many people take their security online for granted, and some even naively assume that they have nothing to lose. As far as cybersecurity is concerned, your data is always valuable to someone. In this realm, there's nothing like worthless data. There's always some useful analytics that someone could extrapolate from your data, so you must take your security seriously.

So, how do corporate entities approach security?

Well, it's quite simple, they have multiple backup solutions. They understand that even with their robust security protocols, anything that could go wrong is possible. With that in mind, they always have routine backups running. This gives them an upper hand in the event of a cyber attack, such that even as they work round the clock to contain the situation, they can still keep their business up and running.

Now, let's bring that concept into perspective.

Imagine yourself in a similar situation. Say your phone or laptop has been infiltrated by a hacker, or let's use an example most people can relate to—you tried to install a program or app that malfunctioned and crashed your system. When your system crashes, in most cases, the only solution is to wipe it clean and start afresh. This means you lose everything, from your contacts, photos, videos, messages, unique app settings, game saves, and so on. Physically, your device is sound and will work like a new one. However, you can imagine the frustration of losing all your data, and how far it sets you back.

But, if you have backups in place, you don't have to worry about that. All you need to do is wipe the device clean, then reinstall the most recent backup and you'll be good to go. I'll give you two simple examples when backups come in handy.

First, we have Google contacts. Google synchronizes your contacts to your account. When you buy a new phone, all you have to do is sign into your account and Google automatically populates your contact list from your most recent backup.

Another example is WhatsApp. If you set up periodic backups, you don't lose your chats when you install WhatsApp on a new device. You simply select the backup file and the app will restore to that point, bringing back all your chats, photos, and videos.

For your computers, if anything ever happens and corrupts your operating system, you could simply roll back changes to the previous backup. Therefore, if you installed a buggy program and your system crashes, you simply go back in time to the moment before you installed that program, and proceed like nothing happened.

Such is the importance of backups. Think of it like insurance. It gives you peace of mind, knowing that if anything ever happens to your devices, you'll have a reasonable reprieve. More importantly, and like the insurance principle of indemnity, having a backup plan restores you to the point you were before the risk occurred.

You can do everything possible to avoid a cyber attack, but at times even the best efforts fail. If this ever happens to you, data backup and recovery is the way to go.

Data Backups. Why Do They Matter?

Data backup means creating an archive or a copy of your valuable information, usually in a separate location, so you can use it at a later date for restoration purposes in case your data is compromised in any way, or you lose it altogether. You've heard the phrase data is the new gold. Thus, in this digital generation, data is one of the most valuable assets you have, and losing it could have far-reaching effects. Here are some reasons why you should perform periodic data backups from time to time:

- Backups allow you to restore your operations as soon as possible, in the event of a breach or any incident that results in irrecoverable loss of data.
- It gives you peace of mind by preempting and protecting you from complete loss of data.
- Backups are an essential part of a digital disaster mitigation and preparedness strategy.
- For business purposes, you can use backups for archiving purposes, especially for record-keeping.

Whether you're running a business or for your personal needs, data backups make a big difference in your digital lifestyle. They give you peace of mind, so you never have to worry about losing your work.

Consequences of A Life Without Backups

It's quite interesting that a lot of people go through life without digital backups. Some don't even know what they are, or why they need them. You probably know at least one person who keeps complaining about losing their data when they buy a new phone and starting afresh each time. In this age and time, that's the closest thing to living precariously, risks that you should never take.

According to World Backup Day, more than 30% of computers in the world are compromised by malware. On top of that, more than 100 phones are stolen every minute. That's six thousand people losing phones every hour. What this means is that more than 60 million phones end up in the hands of criminals each year.

Looking at these statistics, you should strongly consider a backup strategy because you never know when your devices will be stolen or compromised. Even if you have insurance for your phone or computer, they can only replace the device, but not your data.

Without backups, you could fall victim to any of the following risks:

- Phishing attacks
- Human error or accidental data loss
- Negligence
- Ransomware
- Software corruption
- Theft
- Hardware failure

Data loss can disrupt your life in a professional and personal capacity. The magnitude of damage from unauthorized access could be anything from reputational damage to loss of business because of unmitigated downtime, breach of data privacy laws, loss of customer loyalty and trust, and in some cases, contravening compliance laws. Clearly, there's more to this than just losing access to data, your integrity is also on the line.

Types of Backup and Storage

Building on your knowledge of the possible risks of not having backups, we now explore the different options you have. You'll realize that there are lots of backup solutions you could use at any given point and for different reasons. While you could use all of them, it becomes unnecessarily expensive, so choose a solution that's relevant to your immediate needs, and fits your budget. Here's a run-down of your backup and storage options, and how they work:

- **External Hard Drive**

External drives are portable and available in different sizes, so you can conveniently store data in a single external drive or multiple, depending on your needs. You simply plug the external drive into your computer or phone through the USB cable, select the files you wish to save, and transfer them to the drive.

While portability is a good thing, it's also a potential downside for external storage because your drive could easily be stolen. Apart from that, there's the risk of physical damage if the drive falls, which could make your files irrecoverable. Since they plug in and out of devices, all it takes is access to an infected computer to destroy your files.

- **Backup Software**

These are dedicated backup solutions specifically meant to help you select and save your desired files. The good thing about using backup software is that you can create automatic backup schedules, so you don't have to go through the rigors of manually selecting files and backup locations. On top of that, most backup software solutions generally in the market encrypt your data, further strengthening your security.

- **Tape Backup**

This option is perfect for large amounts of data, so it would be relevant for your business, and not personal needs. For example, tapes like the Linear Tape-Open 8 (LTO-8) can hold up to 9 terabytes of data. There are two steps involved. First, you copy data to the tape, and second, you move the tapes to a secure, remote location.

Now, while tape backups can be useful for your business data, one of the challenges is that you cannot recover a single file from the tape. You'd have to recover the entire batch of data, for example, a whole 9 terabytes then skim through to find the single file you needed.

- **Cloud Backup**

Your data is stored in a remote location, but you can easily access it online. Cloud backup is convenient, and in most cases, synchronizes your data as long as you have an internet connection, so your backup is always updated with every change you make on your computer. This is why a lot of people love backup solutions like Dropbox and Google Drive.

- **Removable Media**

This solution is not quite common these days, but some people still prefer it. You store files in removable media like DVDs, USB drives, and CDs. Unfortunately, you are limited by the size of the removable media, for example, most CDs can only hold 700 MB, while most DVDs hold up to 4 GB. Another downside of using removable media is their vulnerability and suscepti-bility to loss and physical damage.

Types of Backup

Let's say you've already selected your desired backup solution. What kind of backup should you perform? Note that your option could be influenced by the file size, duration of time, or any other relevant resource constraints. Let's now look at the six backup types you could consider:

Full Backup

This is the most common, easiest, and most comprehensive type of backup to perform because it saves everything. You're essentially cloning your device.

The good thing with this approach is that restoration is as simple as the backup process because you don't have to go through a rigorous selection process. The downside of using this method is that it could consume a lot of time and space depending on the size of your device.

You can perform the following types of full backups for your devices:

- **Incremental Backup**

This is where you save changes made to your device since the last time you performed a backup. Therefore, after the first full backup, subsequent backups only record changes made to your device after the original backup.

It would be wise to perform a new full backup after a series of incremental backups, so you have a more recent backup foundation to work with if you ever need a restore point.

- **Differential Backup**

This kind of backup is almost similar to the incremental backup. However, the difference is that instead of capturing changes since the most recent backup, it records changes since the most recent full backup.

Thus, you can only perform this after a full backup, taking up less storage space than the full backup, and the recovery or restoration process will also be faster. Compared to incremental backups, however, differential backups consume more space and are slower.

- **Mirror Backup**

This backup process mirrors everything that happens in the original file location. If you copy or delete a file to your device, the same thing happens in the backup folder. This is more or less what happens when you backup files on Dropbox.

Note, however, that most mirror backup service providers offer a 30-day grace period for deleted files. This way, if you delete a file by mistake, you can easily restore it. However, after 30 days, the file is deleted from the server, and you can no longer get it back. It would be wise, therefore, to actively monitor your files, and more importantly, the trash folder in your mirror backup location.

Full PC Backup

It's easy to confuse this with the full backup. While a full backup involves copying and saving files, a full PC backup keeps a record of your PC's architecture at the point of backup.

While a full backup or any other backup will store your documents and other media files, a full PC backup captures an image of the computer, such that when you activate the restore point, your computer is recovered back to the same state it was before the backup, complete with system settings, preferences and any other customizations you might have performed.

The best thing about this is that since it captures an image of the entire system, it will also save your protected or hidden files, which you could easily forget when using other backup types.

Now, while this approach gives you peace of mind, there's the risk of restoring malware and any other issues that might have plagued your system before the backup. On top of that, this approach restores your system to its unique structure. Therefore, you might not be able to restore your computer to a different operating system, or if you changed the motherboard, display adapter, or made any other hardware changes.

Local Backup

This backup approach derives its name from the proximity to the backup file. Once you create the backup, it's stored either in the same office or the same building, making it easier to access for restoration purposes.

It's quite easy to restore the backups since all you have to do is plug the external drive in or connect the host computer and the backup device through a local network.

On the flip side, keeping your backups within the same local area as the original is quite risky, since they both are vulnerable to the same risks.

Offsite Backup

This backup is similar to the local option we discussed above. The difference is in the location. The backup will always be in a different physical location than the source device. You will first perform a local backup, and then once that is done, you move the backup device to a different location, hence the name offsite.

While offsite backups offer an additional layer of protection by physical distance, they can be cumbersome since someone has to physically move the backup to the offsite location each time. Apart from that, you also have to factor in the cost of physical storage and mitigate the risk of damage or theft while the backup is in transit.

Remote Backup

This concept is an offshoot of the offsite backup we discussed above. The difference between the two is that while offsite backups involve physically moving the backup devices, you have an active link to the remote backup site, so you don't need to be physically present to back up or recover your data. You can do it from anywhere in the world.

One of the major challenges of remote backups is the cost. Other than the storage services, the service providers generally charge you for the convenience of being able to store and retrieve your data at will. Besides, since most of the activity takes place online, this solution can be slower than most and is highly dependent on your internet speed

Secure File Transfer Protocol (SFTP) Backup

In this case, your backup is stored on an SFTP server, so everything takes place over the Internet. Like the remote backups above, this is also an advanced version of the offsite backup, since the source data and the backup server are in separate locations.

All you need is an internet connection and a link to the SFTP server to restore your data. Keeping data in separate locations also protects your backups from physical and other types of damage. Unfortunately, you have no control over how fast you can restore data since it comes down to your internet speed, and in some cases, the bandwidth on the backup server side.

Note the difference between SFTP and FTP.

SFTP is a secure network protocol through which you can access, manage, and transfer files online. It is a more secure version of FTP. By default, FTP supports operations at multiple TCP ports (port 20 as the data channel and port 21 as the control channel), which is one of the reasons why hackers can easily penetrate it. On the other hand, SFTP transfers only take place at port 22.

Apart from that, SFTP uses secure shell (SSH) encryption, adding an extra layer of protection to your file management and transfers. The extra security comes at a cost though, as file transfer over SFTP is considerably slower than over FTP. This is because of the additional encryption that isn't present in FTP.

For your security, it's advisable to avoid FTP altogether. You'd rather put up with relatively slow file transfers than risk the exposure of your credentials and sensitive info to prying eyes.

Setting up Your Digital Lifelines

There are different backup solutions you can implement for your digital lifeline. To find the most appropriate one of them all, here are crucial factors you should take into consideration:

- Cost - Can you afford the backup solution? Consider the payment plans, whether it's a one-time payment or periodic recurring payments.
- Space - How much space is sufficient for all your data?
- Ease - An ideal backup solution should be easy to use. From setting up backups to data retrieval, the process

shouldn't be too complicated for you. The simpler it is, the easier and faster it is for you to store your data.

- Security - The whole point of data backups is peace of mind. Make sure your backup options guarantee you different levels of security
- Speed - This goes hand in hand with ease of backup. An ideal backup solution should save your data as fast as possible, and similarly, make the retrieval process seamless. The longer it takes, the higher your risk of the process stalling midway, or failing for any number of reasons.

Backup Scheduling Guidelines

Guided by the factors above, you should have narrowed down your backup options to one or two top contenders, and then select a winner from there. Your next step is backup scheduling. Here are three crucial tips to guide you:

- **Backup Frequency**

How often should you create backups? There's no one-size-fits-all approach here because backup needs vary from one person to the next. That being said, the backup frequency will depend on your immediate needs, the inherent value you bestow on the data in question, and the size. Ideally, you should back up your data once a week. However, depending on your needs, you could also do this once a week, once a month, or every couple of days.

- **Location**

Where will you store the saved data? Security should be your top priority at this point. At the same time, you must also consider convenience. How easy is it for you to save and retrieve the data? Picture a situation where you need to perform an urgent restoration.

- **Timeframe**

Finally, consider the duration of time you wish to have your data stored. This comes down to costs. The longer your data is held somewhere, the higher your costs will be. You could mitigate this by setting up your physical backups in DVDs, hard drives, or thumb drives. Depending on the backup size, you can also upload them to various cloud storage platforms like Google Drive and Dropbox.

How to Backup Data

Having considered the backup scheduling guidelines above, let's now explore how to go about it. For your backup plan to be effective, you must create a plan you'll follow religiously. A commonly recommended plan is the 3-2-1 approach. This strategy aims to ensure that each backup instance creates three safe copies of your data. Here's how it works:

3 - Create Three Copies

For every backup instance, ensure you have three copies; two duplicates and the original file. This way, you'll always be safe if you lose either of the backup files or if your data happens to be corrupted and can no longer be recovered.

2 - Use Two Types of Storage

It's always wise to store backups in two different kinds of storage. The goal here is to mitigate potential loss through failure or other kinds of redundancy in either of the storage options. For example, you can store the files in an external drive, an internal drive, other kinds of removable media, or cloud storage. Note that while this approach recommends two types of storage, there's nothing wrong with using more if you can. At the end of the day, the goal is to make sure your backups are safe.

1 - Keep One Copy Remotely

Strengthen your backup security apparatus by keeping at least one copy offline, in a remote location. Now, this doesn't necessarily mean shipping it off to a CIA black site, or a remote storage facility in Antarctica. All you have to do is ensure that you always have a copy that is not connected to the internet, or the primary device from which the backups were created in the first place. The goal here is to eliminate any challenges that could arise from having all your backups in one place.

Finally, the 3-2-1 approach is often recommended by cybersecurity experts as it provides a credible framework or guideline that you can implement when you're just starting out. It's quite effective in protecting you, not only from criminal threats like malware and ransomware but also from accidental loss, which could happen to anyone. At the end of the day, however, your ideal backup approach should always be guided by your immediate needs. 3-2-1 is a good place to start, but if need be, you can modify or adjust it accordingly.

For more useful insight on secure backups and storage, here's some useful insight from the U.S. Geological Survey (USGS).

Interactive Element

Q1. Why do you need regular backups?

Regular backups give you room to recover information in case of accidental deletion, hardware failure, cyber-attacks, or natural disasters. They also guarantee business continuity by reducing downtime and minimizing the impact of data loss on operations.

Q2. How do you restore data from backups?

There are three processes involved in restoring data from a backup:

- Identify the type and location of the backup containing the needed data.

- Retrieve the backup and restore it to its original location or on a new system.
- Verifying the integrity of the recovered data to ensure it's usable and consistent with the original information.

Q3. What kind of risks do you face if you don't use backups?

You could face any or all of the following challenges if you do not backup your data regularly:

- Costs associated with data recovery efforts, potential revenue loss due to interrupted business operations, and potential fines for failing to protect sensitive information.
- Downtime caused by the unavailability of critical data will affect your operations and productivity.
- Permanent loss of important files or information.

Conclusion

The internet has long been touted as the infrastructure that transformed the world into a global village. It's hard to imagine a time when there was no internet. You'd have to go back several decades back for that. What's even more interesting about the internet is the pace at which it has evolved. Things happen so fast, that most of the current generation can't fathom archived photos of the formative years of products like Windows XP.

It would be unfair to compare the internet we have today with what we had in the 90s and early 2000s. The comparisons might even be worlds apart once we've fully embraced the promise of the metaverse concept, widely considered the next phase in the evolution of the internet as we know it. However, one thing that's remained constant throughout these evolutionary phases is the imminence of threats online.

As the internet evolves, so does the immediate value we derive from it. There was a time when most people would come online to read articles and send emails. Today, you can run a business online, receive money, and transfer it to your bank account in seconds. You can create an entire syllabus and teach courses online. You can play multiplayer video games with your friends in a different part of the world. All this is possible because the internet infrastructure keeps evolving to meet our dynamic needs.

While we enjoy the benefits of this growth, so do the criminal elements that lurk online. Today, cybercrime gets a lot of attention because of the massive threats they pose, and the widespread destructive impact of some of the successful attacks. Cybercrime, unfortunately, is not a new problem. It's a vice that has existed since the early days of the internet and has enjoyed tremendous growth over the years.

We're not the only ones who enjoy the improved efficiency brought about by the evolution of the internet, criminals do too. They look forward to tech advancements just the same way you'd wish to install the latest graphics card on your computer at home or in the office as soon as they are released. The difference is that while you tap into this efficiency for a better computing experience, criminals deploy the same equipment to get better at exploiting your vulnerabilities. A powerful computer, for example, means faster processing, better streaming experience, and maybe smooth rendering depending on what you're using it for. For a criminal, a powerful computer means it's easier to try and hack more accounts faster. So, we're all using the same computing resources, but for different reasons.

One thing you realize about cybersecurity is that threats keep evolving. At a personal level, it's not possible to keep up with this pace, and that's why you should know how to mitigate possible threats around you.

I wrote this book drawing from decades of service in the cyber-security industry. Digital threats are as dynamic as customer tastes and preferences. You can never tell what threat you'll face tomorrow or in the next hour, but one certain thing is that there are, and will always be threats all over the internet.

If you're going to outsmart cybercriminals, you must learn not just how to protect your devices, but how to think like a criminal. This is why we delved into the psychology of crime earlier in the book, giving you insight into the way criminals think. Awareness is always key to mitigating any threats, whether online or even the local threats in your neighborhood. After all, you cannot protect yourself from something you don't know, right? So, at the end of this book, I hope that you are more enlightened about common online threats like ransomware, phishing attacks, and malware. The more you know about them, the easier it gets to identify possible attacks and protect yourself.

As the internet evolves through the metaverse, there will be more threats. While we cannot convincingly predict what kind of threats they will be, the same threats we face today may just morph into iterations capable of frustrating users in the meta-verse. This is why awareness is key.

This is the age of data, and there are lots of companies, websites, programs, and apps that work day and night to get a hold of yours. Whether they do this legitimately or not, is a story for another day. However, everyone is after your data, especially the most important one of them all, your digital identity. Recognizing the immense value of your data, especially in the wrong hands, you must be cautious, and viciously protect your data.

Over the years, I've come to appreciate the role of preventive mechanisms in cybersecurity. It is true when they say prevention is better than cure. Whether at a personal or professional level, make sure you deploy sufficient preventive solutions to safeguard your digital lifestyle. I'm talking about simple things like using encryption services on digital products where possible, using MFA on accounts that support it, making sure your software and apps are always updated, and so on. These are things we often take for granted, but they go a long way in strengthening your defenses. On top of that, create a culture of consciousness and awareness of cybersecurity threats, challenges, and innovations.

Technology is amazing. However, technology can be redundant without human intervention. Technology, on its own, cannot serve and protect us effectively. Despite your ability to deploy various security features, you must still make the big calls. Ultimately, your security online comes down to your discernment, judgment, awareness, and mindfulness. You must embrace an inquisitive mindset, where you verify sources before you engage someone online. You must implement a healthy digital routine to outsmart criminals, and more importantly, get into the habit of reporting vulnerabilities as soon as you encounter them. If we can get a lot more people doing this, cybersecurity easily becomes a collective approach to creating a healthy and resilient digital ecosystem where everyone is aware of their responsibility and takes it seriously. This is also how we protect the vulnerable in our society like kids and the elderly from being exploited by criminals.

Finally, I hope this book equips you with not only knowledge of cybersecurity and the threats around you, but also to instill a proactive, resilient, and vigilant mindset in you so that you understand and appreciate the important role you play in digital security from a bigger-picture perspective. Impenetrable security might be elusive, but you can easily fortify your security apparatus by learning and adapting to the evolving threatscape.

Moving forward, carry the lessons you've learned in this book, and share them with your loved ones. Implement the strategies we discussed where you can, and together, we can take steps towards building the kind of online experience we can all be proud of. Remember, the future of cybersecurity isn't limited to technology and how we use it, but in the collective efforts we invest in establishing online communities that will thrive beyond our wildest imagination.

References

Arctic Wolf. (2022, November 16). *History of Cybercrime | Arctic Wolf.* Arctic Wolf. https://arcticwolf.com/resources/blog/decade-of-cybercrime/

Australian Signals Directorate. (2021, September 23). *Business email compromise | Cyber.gov.au.* Cyber.gov.au. https://www.cyber.gov.au/threats/types-threats/business-email-compromise

Bhadwal, A. (2023). *The History of Cyber Security: A Detailed Guide [Infographic].* Knowledgehut.com. https://www.knowledgehut.com/blog/security/history-of-cyber-security

Buchanan Technologies. (2022, May 17). *4 Reasons Why Cybersecurity is Important.* Buchanan Technologies. https://www.buchanan.com/why-cybersecurity-important/

Carpenter, P. (2022, April 21). Council Post: Five Cognitive Biases That Can Threaten Your Cybersecurity Efforts. *Forbes.* https://www.forbes.com/sites/forbesbusinesscouncil/2021/12/30/five-cognitive-biases-that-can-threaten-your-cybersecurity-efforts/?sh=8bfb1619e319

Cassetto, O. (2023, February 1). *Cybersecurity Threats: Types and Challenges - Exabeam.* Exabeam. https://www.exabeam.com/information-security/cyber-security-threat/

Cisa. (2023, January 17). *Cyber Threats and Advisories | Cybersecurity and Infrastructure Security Agency CISA.* Cisa.gov. https://www.cisa.gov/topics/cyber-threats-and-advisories

Cisco. (2023, October). *What Is Social Engineering in Cyber Security?* Cisco. https://www.cisco.com/c/en/us/products/security/what-is-social-engineering.html

Computer Security Resource Center. (2015). *Cyber Threat - Glossary | CSRC.* Nist.gov. https://csrc.nist.gov/glossary/term/cyber_threat

CoreTech. (2022). *6 Motivations of Cyber Criminals.* Coretech.us. https://www.coretech.us/blog/6-motivations-of-cyber-criminals

Creese, S., Dutton, W. H., & Esteve-González, P. (2021). The social and cultural shaping of cybersecurity capacity building: a comparative study of nations and regions. *Personal and Ubiquitous Computing, 25*(5), 941–955. https://doi.org/10.1007/s00779-021-01569-6

Farrier, E. (2023, July 20). *What is social engineering? Definition + protection tips.* Norton. https://us.norton.com/blog/emerging-threats/what-is-social-engineering

Giannelis, M. (2022, May 3). *Tech Business News.* Tech Business News. https://www.techbusinessnews.com.au/blog/impact-of-the-internet-on-modern-society/

IBM. (2023). *What is a cyberattack? | IBM.* Ibm.com. https://www.ibm.com/topics/cyber-attack

Imperva. (2023, October 7). *Cybersecurity Threats | Types & Sources | Imperva.* Learning Center. https://www.imperva.com/learn/application-security/cyber-security-threats/

Internet Crime Complaint Center. (2018). *Internet Crime Complaint Center(IC3) | Home Page.* Ic3.Gov. https://www.ic3.gov/

Kaspersky. (2013, December 6). *History of malicious programs.* Kaspersky.com; Kaspersky. https://encyclopedia.kaspersky.com/knowledge/history-of-malicious-programs/

Kelley, K. (2020, May 29). *What is Cybersecurity and Why It is Important?* Simplilearn.com; Simplilearn. https://www.simplilearn.com/tutorials/cyber-security-tutorial/what-is-cyber-security

Marroquin, J. (2019, September 23). *The CyberCrimes Triangle.* Linkedin.com. https://www.linkedin.com/pulse/cybercrimes-triangle-jose-marroquin-joe-/

Microsoft Security Team. (2020, June 30). *The psychology of social engineering— the "soft" side of cybercrime | Microsoft Security Blog.* Microsoft Security Blog. https://www.microsoft.com/en-us/security/blog/2020/06/30/psychol ogy-social-engineering-soft-side-cybercrime/

Olmstead, K., & Smith, A. (2017, March 22). *What the Public Knows About Cybersecurity.* Pew Research Center: Internet, Science & Tech. https://www.pewresearch.org/internet/2017/03/22/what-the-public-knows-about-cybersecurity/

Outsource Accelerator. (2022, February 28). *Improving cybersecurity in the era of remote working.* Outsource Accelerator; Outsource Accelerator. https://www.outsourceaccelerator.com/articles/cybersecurity-in-remote-work/

Palatty, N. J. (2023, April 18). *How Many Cyber Attacks Per Day: The Latest Stats and Impacts in 2023.* Astra Security Blog. https://www.getastra.com/blog/security-audit/how-many-cyber-attacks-per-day/#:

Quotefancy. (2023). *Sun Tzu Quote: "Against those skilled in attack, an enemy does not know where to defend; against the experts in defense, the enemy does ..."* Quotefancy.com. https://quotefancy.com/quote/1548485/Sun-Tzu-Against-those-skilled-in-attack-an-enemy-does-not-know-where-to-defend-against

Ranjan, A. (2019, June 25). *Cyber Criminals and its Types.* GeeksforGeeks; GeeksforGeeks. https://www.geeksforgeeks.org/cyber-criminals-and-its-types/

Raza, M. (2023, February 13). *Social Engineering Attacks: The 4 Stage Lifecycle & Common Techniques.* Splunk-Blogs; Splunk. https://www.splunk.com/en_us/blog/learn/social-engineering-attacks.html

Sachs, D. (2023, June 6). *The Tricky Mind Games of Cognitive Biases in Information Security.* Cybersecuritytribe.com. https://www.cybersecuritytribe.com/articles/the-tricky-mind-games-of-cognitive-biases-in-information-security

Spanning Cloud Apps. (2022, June 30). *Cybersecurity Awareness: Definition, Importance & More | Spanning.* Spanning. https://spanning.com/blog/cyber security-awareness/

Statista. (2023). *Time spent online worldwide 2023 | Statista.* Statista; Statista. https://www.statista.com/statistics/1380282/daily-time-spent-online-global/#:

Visma. (2018). *Why is cyber security important | Cyber security.* Visma.com. https://www.visma.com/cyber-security/why-is-cyber-security-important/

Yehezkel, S. (2022, June 30). *"Know your enemy," and other cybersecurity lessons from Sun Tzu's Art of War.* Cyber Defense Magazine. https://www.cyberdefensemagazine.com/know-your-enemy/

Printed in Great Britain
by Amazon

45101871R00145